EFFECTIVE BIBLICAL COUNSELING

Lawrence J. Crabb Jr.

Ministry Resources Library

Zondervan Publishing House • Grand Rapids, MI

EFFECTIVE BIBLICAL COUNSELING: A Model for Helping
Caring Christians Become Capable Counselors

Copyright © 1977 by The Zondervan Corporation

Requests for information should be addressed to:
Zondervan Publishing House
Academic and Professional Books
Grand Rapids, Michigan 49530

ISBN 0-310-22570-1

"Published in assocation with the literary agency of Sealy M. Yates and
associates, Orange, California."

Library of Congress Cataloging in Publication Data
Crabb, Lawrence J.
    Effective biblical counseling.
    1. Christianity—Psychology.   2. Counseling.   I. Title.
BR110.C76   253.5   77-2146

Printed in the United States of America

    93 94 95 96 / AF / 31 30 29

This edition is printed on acid-free paper and meets the American National
Standards Institute Z39.48 standard.

To Rachael

PART I: A FEW PRELIMINARIES

EFFECTIVE
BIBLICAL
COUNSELING

Contents

Preface

Referring to some of our more modern church music, my father once wrote to me, "I think we so often sing silliness, almost as though we are attempting to delude ourselves with the thought that the Christian life is a ball." No Christian who is seriously trying to pursue the knowledge of Christ routinely experiences the frothy, bubbly, giddy sort of joy which so often is held out as the normal Christian life. Everyone has real and intense personal struggles which dedication to Christ does not eliminate. The harsh truth is that living for the Lord sometimes increases the severity of the struggle.

The struggles we experience have several causes. Some of our suffering is the inevitable lot of fallen people living in a fallen world. The results of the Fall include separation not only from God and from others, but also from ourselves. We "come apart" as persons, unable to genuinely accept ourselves as we are. Our consequent struggle to be or to pretend to be what we are not explains much of our deep discontent and personal suffering. Becoming a Christian does not end the struggle; it provides us with the resources to see the battle through to a successful conclusion. Some of our suffering is the direct result of being a Christian (Rom. 8:17). The Lord often allows His people to suffer as a means of promoting an awareness of His absolute sufficiency. Sometimes our suffering is related to unbiblical patterns of living. Whatever the cause, people today are wrestling with personal distress and afflictions.

I believe that God has ordained the local church as His primary instrument to tend to our personal aches and pains. We must admit that, generally speaking, we are not doing a very good job in this area. In writing this book I have tried to be of practical help to Christians who want to be more effective in ministering to their suffering brothers and sisters. I therefore asked a few Christians who care about people to read the manuscript and to let me know if I was communicating to them. Like the child who guarantees a positive response by asking his aunts, cousins, and grandparents to buy tickets to his school play, I first solicited comments on my book from my father, Lawrence Crabb, Sr., and brother, William Crabb, both of whom I deeply respect as committed, knowledgeable, mature Christians. I thank them both for their thoughts. Let me pass on a reaction expressed by my father:

"One sad thought kept recurring as I read this book, written on the assumption that believers care for one another, an assumption which we *must* make in order to advocate a course of action such as you recommend. Paul seems in tears as he speaks in Philippians 2:21. 'For all seek their own, not the things which are Jesus Christ's.' Self and self-centeredness are the most prevalent and despicable factors inhibiting the growth of the church. We must realize that Christian service is not only evangelizing but includes the selfless building up of the Lord's people. Perhaps this is the most important aspect of service since a healthy group of believers best illustrates the Body of Christ and has a magnetic influence far greater than a fervent gospel appeal. Israel was to be a separate, peculiar people, illustrating the power of God to guide and govern a nation. In so doing they were to be a light to the Gentiles. Instead their conduct caused the name of God to be

Preface

blasphemed among the Gentiles." Many other comments as well, some on particular portions of the book, increased my already deep respect and appreciation for my father.

The comments offered by my brother Bill also were unusually helpful. As brothers by birth, brothers by rebirth, and brothers by common interest (he is currently involved in graduate counselor training), we enjoy an ongoing dialogue about biblical counseling.

Rev. David Nicholas, a good friend and the effective pastor of Spanish River Presbyterian Church, deserves my special thanks not only for his critique of the manuscript but also for providing me with the opportunity to test some of my thinking in a local congregation.

I also want to thank two colleagues, Dr. Linda Murphy and Dr. Jerry Gill, who faithfully counsel according to Scripture and who encourage me in my ministry, for their helpful response to this book.

The typing and proofreading responsibilities were effectively handled by my secretary, Bebby Weigand. Anyone who can decipher my scrawl and does so without complaining deserves a public thank you.

And to my family, a super wife and two great kids (Keppy and Kenny), a big thank you for putting up with an often preoccupied husband and father.

Lawrence J. Crabb, Jr., Ph.D.
Boca Raton, Florida

11

Introduction

In my first book, *Basic Principles of Biblical Counseling* (Zondervan, 1975), I developed in rather broad outline an approach to counseling which I believe to be psychologically sound and consistent with Scripture. The book offers the philosophical and conceptual thinking on which I build my counseling approach. Although the careful reader will notice a number of shifted emphases between the first book and this one, the basic concepts remain largely unchanged. My purpose in writing this volume is to think through a model of counseling which can be gracefully integrated into the functioning of the local church. In my view, any approach to counseling which is truly biblical will work most effectively when carried out in the context of a local body of believers. We hear much these days about such concepts as body life, koinonia fellowship, and agape love. The emphasis is not only biblical but also timely for a Christian church which has become largely impersonal and superficial in its practice of community.

Effective body life however produces its own problems. When Christians begin to experience the thrill of true acceptance

13

and begin to taste the possibilities of deep fellowship both with the Lord and each other, it often happens that long and deeply hidden problems begin to surface. Local bodies must not at that point *routinely* tell their brothers and sisters who are hurting to seek professional help. We must provide alternative resources for dealing with these problems *within the body* where people can benefit from the healing potential inherent in body functioning while they receive appropriate counseling help. Counseling and life in the body should not be separated. The job before us is to develop a model of biblical counseling which can be integrated gracefully into the local church. My goal in this book is to outline such a model and to explore a few preliminary ideas on strategies for integration.

Counseling is not a discipline like dentistry or medicine which depends fundamentally upon a growing amount of technical knowledge administered by a highly trained professional. Rather, counseling is centrally and critically a relationship between people who care. As with most concepts, we can err by falling off either side of the narrow platform of truth. Some insist that counseling is *no more* than relationship. I disagree. There are technical understandings of psychological dynamics and therapeutic procedure which add greatly to counseling effectiveness. Others fall off the opposite side, insisting that counseling is the scientific enterprise of applying experimentally proven laboratory truths to modify troublesome behavior. But when we consider that man is a personal creature made in God's image and is intended for fellowship with God, we recognize that counseling which de-emphasizes the interpersonal dimensions of trust, care, and acceptance cannot be truly effective.

Since effective counseling requires both a caring relationship and an understanding of human functioning, we need to find mature believers in our local churches who are filled with the love of Christ and train them in counseling insights and skills. This book is dedicated to the proposition that caring, mature Christian people (who can love because they know Christ's love and who are mature because they desire above all else to know Him) can

14

become capable counselors within their local church bodies.

I suppose that some professionally trained counselors will feel threatened by such thinking or perhaps will dismiss it as ignorant optimism. I appeal to them to consider the untapped potential for healing if the above proposition is true. In dealing with distressed people, counselors who are part of the same local church and who therefore know the members will be able to mobilize resources of friendship, care, practical helps, and prayer in the service of their clients. In my view, we professionals still will be needed but our role will change. No longer will we be the high priests of that mysterious, inner-sanctum world of psychotherapy. The private practice model invites people to leave the folks who know and care for them to go to the professional and pay for his love and skill. In the model I am proposing, many people will turn to each other and to leaders we have trained to find biblical answers to their problems. Counselors who are a part of the local body will be able to draw intelligently upon the resources of a caring, supportive community to help meet the needs of their "clients."

The function of Christian professionals will be twofold: (1) train gifted Christians in the local church to counsel and (2) offer backup resources where needed. I do not agree with the opinion of some that psychologists should close their doors and refer people to their ministers. Although the Scriptures provide the only authoritative information on counseling, psychology and its specialized discipline of psychotherapy offer some valid insights about human behavior which in no way contradict Scripture. If we combine these insights with the healing resources of a local body of caring, committed Christians by training people in the church to handle a good deal of the counseling load, we might witness a tremendous increase in spiritual and emotional maturity in our churches.

Three Kinds of Counseling

Every Christian is called to a ministry of encouraging and helping others, especially those in the household of faith. We do

15

not need more conferences and books on esoteric issues of counseling theory; we need to challenge, encourage, and assist members of local churches to get on with the job of one-anothering: love one another, bear one another's burden, pray for one another. Encouragement is one kind of a counseling ministry available to every Christian. Pastors, elders, and other church leaders have special opportunity and responsibility to teach biblical principles of living. That is a second kind of counseling. Some need to be specifically trained for a specialized ministry of counseling involving deeper exploration into stubborn problems. This is a third kind of counseling and is the major concern of this book.

In my effort to communicate a biblical model of counseling, I have suggested ideas about how people function which any Christian can understand and use in a practical way to handle his own personal problems and to help others in dealing with their concerns. Although some of the material is a bit technical, it is generally written in a jargon-free and hopefully readable style which people with no academic training in counseling can follow. It is my hope that each of us as members of the living body of Christ will become more sensitive to ourselves and to each other and will develop an effective ministry in appropriating the sufficiency of Christ to heal the pain we discover. May God bless this book to the end that counseling in the local church soon will become a reality.

CHAPTER 1

The Goal of Counseling: What Are We Trying to Do?

Are We Really Being Selfish?.

Listen to what might be a typical conversation between a client and a Christian counselor:

Client: "I am so frustrated. I feel like I'm going to explode. There must be some way to calm down. If one more thing goes wrong, I'm going to go crazy."

Counselor: "Sounds like you're feeling pretty desperate."

Client: "I really am desperate. Even though I am a Christian and I do believe the Bible, nothing is working. I've tried praying, confessing, giving, repenting, everything. There must be an answer in God but I can't find it."

Counselor: "I share your convictions that the Lord can bring peace. Let's look to see what may be blocking His work in your life."

Counseling at this point might follow one of many avenues, depending on the theoretical persuasions of the counselor, the

19

nature of the relationship with the client, and a host of other factors. Whatever direction counseling may take, think carefully for a moment about the *goal*. What is the client ultimately asking for? What is he hoping will happen above all else as a result of his counseling? As I listen to many patients and introspect about my own goals when struggling with a personal problem, it seems to me that the usual objective so passionately desired is fundamentally self-centered: "I want to feel good" or "I want to be happy."

Now there is nothing wrong in wanting to be happy. An obsessive preoccupation with "my happiness," however, often obscures our understanding of the biblical route to deep, abiding joy. The Lord has told us that there are pleasures forever at His right hand. If we desire those pleasures, we must learn what it means to be at God's right hand. Paul tells us that Christ has been exalted to God's right hand (Eph. 1:20). It follows naturally that the more I abide in Christ, the more I will enjoy the pleasures available in fellowship with God. If I am to experience true happiness, I must desire above all else to become more like the Lord, to live in subjection to the Father's will as He did.

Many of us place top priority not on becoming Christ like in the middle of our problems but on finding happiness. I want to be happy but the paradoxical truth is that I will never be happy if I am concerned primarily with becoming happy. My overriding goal must be in every circumstance to respond biblically, to put the Lord first, to seek to behave as He would want me to. The wonderful truth is that as we devote all our energies to the task of becoming what Christ wants us to be, He fills us with joy unspeakable and a peace far surpassing what the world offers. I must firmly and consciously by an act of my will reject the goal of becoming happy and adopt the goal of becoming more like the Lord. The result will be happiness for me as I learn to dwell at God's right hand in fellowship with Christ. Our modern emphasis on personal wholeness, human potential, and the freedom to be ourselves has quietly shifted us away from a burning concern for becoming more like the Lord to a more primary interest in our development as persons which, we are implicitly promised, will lead to our happiness.

Look at the titles of so many Christian books today: *The Christian's Secret of a Happy Life; Be All You Can Be; All We're Meant to Be; The Total Woman; The Fulfilled Woman.* Many contain excellent and truly biblical concepts, but their message, whether defined or implied, sometimes directs us more toward concern with self-expression and less toward an interest in conformity to Christ's image. The Bible, however, teaches that if I will obediently abide in truth in order to become more like God and thus make Him known, the by-product will be my eventual happiness. But neither the goal of the Christian life nor the goal of Christian counseling is an individual's happiness. Trying to find happiness is something like trying to fall asleep. As long as you consciously and zealously try to grasp it, it never comes.

Paul said it was his ambition (goal) not to become happy but to please God at every moment. What a transforming thought! When I drive my car to work and someone cuts me off, when my kids act up during church, when the dishwasher breaks — my primary responsibility is to *please God!* In Hebrews 13:15,16, we are told that believer-priests (all of us are priests) have a twofold function: (1) to offer the sacrifice of worship to God and (2) to offer the sacrifice of service for others. If I want to please God at every moment, I must be centrally occupied with worship and service. It seems to me that a seriously neglected truth in most Christian counseling efforts is this: the basic biblical reason for wanting to solve your personal problem should be that you want to enter into a deeper relationship with God, to more effectively please Him through worship and service.

Personally rewarding dividends are provided in abundance. Paul was greatly strengthened in his afflictions by the prospect of heaven. He looked forward to the wonderful rest and undisturbed joy he is this moment experiencing. I presume he has been having a great time for the last nineteen hundred years getting to know the Lord better and enjoying chats with Peter, Luther, and my grandparents among others. He is supremely happy. But personal happiness must be seen as a by-product, not a goal. I am to glorify[1] God and, *as I do so,* I will enjoy Him. I must not rewrite the Westminster Shorter Catechism to read that I am to glorify God *in order to* enjoy Him. That goal of happiness is forever elusive regardless of one's strategy. The by-product of happiness is wonderfully available to those whose goal is to please God at every moment.

The next time you grapple with a personal problem (perhaps right now), ask yourself, "Why do I want to solve this problem?" If the honest answer is, "So I can be happy," you are miles away from the biblical solution. What then can you do? Adopt by a conscious, definite, thunderously decisive act of the will a different goal: "I want to solve this problem in a way that will make me more like the Lord. Then I will be able to worship God more fully and serve Him more effectively." Write it on a three-by-five card. Read it every hour. Reaffirm it regularly even though it feels rather artificial and mechanical. Pray that God will confirm it within you as you continue by an act of the will to assert it. Put your goal into practice in definite ways. Begin to worship Him by thanking Him for what disturbs you most. Look for creative ways to begin serving Him.

Christian counselors must be sensitive to the depths of selfishness resident within human nature. It is frighteningly easy to assist a person to reach a nonbiblical goal. It is our responsibility as fellow members of the body continually to remind and exhort each other to keep in view the goal of all true counseling: *to free people to better worship and serve God* by helping them become more like the Lord. In a word, the goal is maturity.

Spiritual and Psychological Maturity

Paul wrote in Colossians 1:28 that his verbal interaction with people (counseling?) always was designed to promote Christian maturity. Only the maturing believer is entering more deeply into the ultimate purpose of his life, namely, worship and service. Biblical counseling therefore will adopt as its major strategy the promotion of spiritual and psychological maturity. When we talk with other believers, we must always have in our minds the purpose of assisting them to become more mature so they can better please God.

Maturity involves two elements: (1) immediate obedience in specific situations and (2) long-range character growth. In order to understand what I mean by maturity and to see how these two elements contribute to its development, we first must grasp the biblical starting point in our quest for maturity. Nothing is more crucial to an effective Christian life than a clear awareness of its foundation. Christian experience begins with *justification,* the act by which God declares me to be acceptable. If I am to become psychologically whole and spiritually mature, I must understand clearly that my acceptability to God is not based on my behavior but rather on Jesus' behavior (Titus 3:5). He was (and is) perfect. Because He never sinned, He never deserved to die. But He voluntarily went to the cross. His death was the punishment which my sins deserve. In His love He provided for an exchange. When I give Him my sins, He pays for them in order to justly forgive me, then He gives me the gift of His righteousness. God declares me to be righteous on the basis of what Jesus has done for me. I have been declared just. I am justified. It is a gift which God does not put in me (I am still a sinner) but which He declares is now mine. I cannot lose it. I am accepted as I am because my acceptability has nothing to do with how I am or how I was yesterday or how I will be tomorrow. It depends on Jesus' perfection alone.

This point must not be relegated to the dry realm of theology. It is at the heart of all Christian growth and yet many who understand the doctrine of substitutionary atonement fail to see its overwhelming practical application to our lives. Our entire motivation for all our behavior hinges upon this doctrine. Efforts to please God by living as we should and resisting temptation so often are motivated by pressure. We feel some vague sense of dread compulsion spurring us on to obedience. So we obey under threat of something foreboding. Are we afraid of God's wrath?

"There is therefore now no *condemnation* to them which are in Christ Jesus." Are we worried about whether we will be accepted? But our acceptance depends on the atoning work of Christ. Perhaps we fear that His love will be stopped? "Who shall lay any thing to the charge of God's elect?" Nothing "shall be able to separate us from the love of God, which is in Christ Jesus our Lord." Because we worry about these things, not really believing the Scripture, we tend to look to other Christians for confirmation of our acceptability. Their approval becomes too important, so we try to please them in order to gain their approval. At that point we begin to feel pressure from them to measure up. When we don't satisfy what we believe are their expectations, we feel guilty and avoid them or deceive them. Fellowship is broken. When we do our best and they show disapproval or fail to praise our efforts, we get angry with them.

So much of our Christian activity is motivated by a personal desire to win someone's approval and hence become acceptable. All the pain and problems which result from that sort of motivation are unnecessary because of the doctrine of justification by faith. I am already acceptable. I don't need anyone's approval. God has declared me to be OK. When I understand that even feebly, my inevitable response is, "Thank You, Lord — I want to please You." Paul said he was constrained not by pressure to be acceptable but rather by the incomprehensible love of Christ (2 Cor. 5:14). His root motivation was love. He wanted to please God and serve men not to become acceptable but because he already was acceptable. The foundation of the entire Christian life then is a proper understanding of justification.

Someday I will be glorified. I will be in heaven. Not until then will all my imperfections be removed. What God has declared to be true, that I am totally acceptable, He one day will make true in my actual being — I will be completely free from all sinful desires, thoughts, and acts. Until that time (which we usually call glorification), God is in the process of sanctifying me, of purifying me, of slowly helping me to become more of what He already has declared me to be. He has granted me the position of acceptability. Now He instructs me to grow up to my position, to behave more and more acceptably. The motivation to do so is love. He has given me the Holy Spirit who tells me how to live and enables me to live that way. Because I am justified, my glorification is certain. I will reveal God's character when I see Him for then I shall be like Him. But God has told me that in the time between my justification and glorification, I am to walk the path of obedience. Christian maturity involves becoming more and more like the Lord Jesus through increased obedience to the Father's will.

Let me sketch what I've said so far.

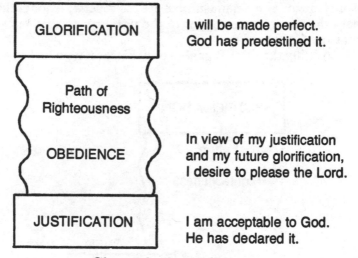

GLORIFICATION	I will be made perfect. God has predestined it.
Path of Righteousness	
OBEDIENCE	In view of my justification and my future glorification, I desire to please the Lord.
JUSTIFICATION	I am acceptable to God. He has declared it.

Chart 1 in Appendix

All who are justified will one day be glorified. Our justification (past) and glorification (future) depend entirely on God alone. But in the interim, we all have a great deal of trouble with obedience. We easily stray from the path of righteousness and do not always follow biblical patterns of behavior. Christian counseling is concerned with whether or not the client is responding obediently to whatever circumstance he is experiencing. Often in counseling it will become clear that the counselee is not responding in a biblical way to stressful circumstances. He may be under terrible strain; there may be a history which makes his present behavior perfectly understandable and natural, and with these problems we can sympathize deeply. Yet we must insist that regardless of circumstances or background, God's faithfulness assures us that the client has all the resources he needs to learn to behave biblically in the present situation. God will never allow a situation to develop in any believer's life to which he cannot respond biblically. As I understand the reality of "Christ in me" through His Spirit, I can never say, "But I can't behave as God wants me to. The circumstances are too much." A counselor must help the client to move over to the pathway of obedience. I call that the OVER goal.

Adding the OVER goal to our sketch, it now looks like this.

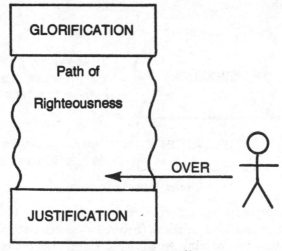

Chart 2 in Appendix

Much of counseling amounts to a clearing away of blocks such as "I can't," "I won't," "I don't know how to handle this." Temptations to which the client regularly yields often are the problem. They require more than exhortations to "do it God's way." Specific methods for resisting temptation which depend on both psychological and spiritual resources will be discussed later. Whatever the approach, the goal is to help the client respond biblically to problem circumstances, to "move over."

Obedience, however, is only one part of the goal. A Christian must do more than change his behavior. Attitudes must change, desires should slowly conform more to God's design, there must be a new style of living which represents more than a collection of obedient responses. The change must be not only external obedience, but also an inward newness, a renewed way of thinking and perceiving, a changed set of goals, a transformed personality. I call this second, broader objective the UP goal. People need to move not only OVER but also UP.

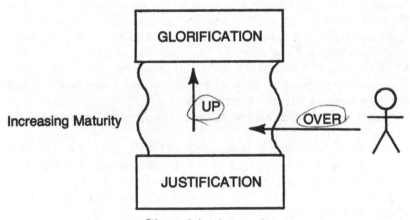

Chart 3 in Appendix

Paul speaks of immature Christians who really do not grasp in a practical moment to moment way the reality of the lordship of Christ. They live in a manner that is not remarkably different from unbelievers. They quarrel, become easily irritated, express jealousies and resentments. They don't get along with each other very well. Those who are mature (or better, those who are becoming increasingly mature) are those who truly understand what the Christian life is all about. In their hearts they want nothing more than to worship and serve Christ. They understand the ultimate goal of Christian living. They stumble and fall, but they quickly repent, get back up and on track again.

Gene Getz has written a helpful book entitled *The Measure of a Man*. The contents essentially represent an operational definition of Christian maturity. When Paul instructed Timothy and Titus to seek out men for leadership positions, he told them to look for certain observable characteristics which taken together reflect maturity. Getz lists twenty measures of maturity and briefly discusses what each one really is and suggests many helpful practical thoughts on how to develop them. These descriptions are useful to a counselor as a guide for promoting and evaluating maturity. In later chapters I will discuss thoroughly the notion that in order to develop maturity, the kind which weathers difficult storms, certain crucial parts of a client's belief system must be identified and directly changed. Behavioral change (the OVER goal) is a necessary prerequisite for maturity, but more fundamental changes in a client's assumptions about what satisfies basic needs like worthwhileness, importance, and security always are helpful and usually are required if stable Christian maturity is to develop.

It should be noted that the goal of OVER and UP is radically different from usual goals set by secular counselors. Ullman and Krasner,[3] two well-known behavioral psychologists have defined humanism as "any system or mode of thought or action in which human interests, values, and dignity predominate." Most psychological theories explicitly or implicitly accept humanistic doctrine as the foundation for their thinking. A system where "human interests, values, and dignity predominate" is unashamedly a man-centered system with no room for the holy direction of an objective and personal God. If, in the therapists' judgment, human interests conflict with biblical injunctions,

Scripture is casually set aside in favor of the higher goal. To the
secularist (and, as was noted earlier, often to the Christian) the
happiness of the client is supreme. Whatever promotes a personal
sense of well-being is desirable. Lazarus,[4] in a generally excellent
and useful book, adopts as his value system a single moral precept
which most secularists would likely embrace: "You are entitled to
do, think and feel whatsoever you please provided no one gets
harmed in the process." Issues of morality are settled quickly
according to this precept with no regard whatsoever for God's
character and revealed law. Let me say quickly, however, that
sensitive secular therapists do *not* necessarily try to change a
person's value system to agree with theirs and they can be
genuinely helpful in dealing with believers, provided the goals of
therapy coincide or at least do not in a given instance conflict with
the general OVER and UP goal.

It must still be said, though, that secular psychology operates
from a radically different set of presuppositions than Christianity
insists upon and the goals for an individual client may be affected
by these differences. For example, a marital adjustment which
contradicts biblical teaching on the roles of husband and wife
would satisfy the secularist but not the Christian. Such an adjustment does not violate the limited humanistic concern for
personal interests, values, or dignity and certainly in no way
harms other people. But the goal of moving OVER to biblical
conformity has not been reached and the goal of pressing UP
toward an attitude of Christlike submission to the Father's will
was never considered (and in most cases would be considered
laughably irrelevant).

Summary

The goal of biblical counseling is to promote Christian
maturity, to help people enter into a richer experience of worship
and a more effective life of service. In broad terms, Christian
maturity is developed by (1) dealing with any immediate problem
circumstances in a manner consistent with Scripture: MOVE
OVER; and (2) developing an inward character which conforms

to the character (attitudes, beliefs, purposes) of Christ: MOVE UP.

Notes

[1]We often use the words "glorify," "glory," "glorious" without stopping to define them clearly. I am indebted to my father for the suggestion that to glorify God is to reveal His essential Being. "Father, the hour is come; glorify (reveal) thy Son, that thy Son also may glorify (reveal) thee" (John 17:1). I glorify God as I reveal Him by walking as He walked.

[2]In the back of the book are easily removed copies of the significant charts throughout the chapters. For ease in following my thinking, you may want to tear out these charts and refer to them as you read without having to thumb back a few pages to look at the chart included in the text. Many of the charts are reproduced in the CHART APPENDIX.

[3]L. Ullmann and L. Krasner, *Case Studies in Behavior Modification* (New York: Holt, Rinehart & Winston, 1965).

[4]A. Lazarus, *Behavior Therapy and Beyond* (New York: McGraw Hill, 1971).

CHAPTER 2

Christianity and Psychology: Enemies or Allies?

Before discussing the strategy involved in helping people move OVER and UP, it may be important to share my views on the thorny, hotly debated, and far from resolved problem of integrating Christianity and psychology. In promoting Christian maturity through counseling, are we permitted to draw from secular psychological theory and procedures? Is it permissible for a Christian counselor's thinking to be shaped or in any way influenced by the work of unbelieving psychologists? Certain secular approaches to helping people such as Transactional Analysis[1] have become popular in evangelical circles. How is a Christian to deal with these positions? Do they offer valid insights from which a Christian can profit or are they in every part unacceptable?

Perhaps many of the personal problems which people bring to counselors are completely unrelated to spiritual issues; for these concerns are the OVER and UP objectives (and for that matter all of Christianity) somewhat irrelevant? How do you promote obedience and character growth in someone who complains of a strong fear of snakes which interferes with family camping trips?

31

Do you discuss his biblical responsibilities to his family and exhort him to go in spite of his fear, trusting God for protection and peace? Or do you use the behaviorist technique of systematic desensitization, a secular technique with fairly well-documented effectiveness? Some would feel that problems like that are parallel to a cavity in your tooth which requires the services of a qualified dentist. The dentist's beliefs about the Lord are far less important to the Christian patient than are his professional skills. Are the various problems which people experience really medical or psychological problems best handled by professional psychotherapists or do they at some level represent a turning away from or an inadequate grasp of spiritual truth?

These questions are important. If psychology offers insights which will sharpen our counseling skills and increase our effectiveness, we want to know them. If all problems are at core spiritual matters we don't want to neglect the critically necessary resources available through the Lord by a wrong emphasis on psychological theory. Because my own thinking on integration is reflected in many of the concepts I will develop later in this book, it seems appropriate to summarize my perspective on an acceptable relationship between secular psychology and biblical truth.

As I read the writings of Christian psychologists, it appears that there are a number of different positions on the matter of integration. The situation is rather like the one prevailing among the various Protestant denominations, where every group claims that its position is truly biblical. The problem facing evangelical Christians who are wrestling with integration is straightforward enough to describe. There is a body of revealed truth in propositional form to which all evangelicals are committed as the inerrant, inspired Word of God. There is another vast literature which represents the diverse, sometimes contradictory, theories and observations which we can call simply secular psychology. Let each be symbolized by a circle. The circle of revealed truth has at the center the person of Christ and His atoning work on the cross.

Buswell, in his *Systematic Theology*, states that the central presupposition of Christianity is Jesus Christ as the second Person of the sovereign, triune Godhead as presented in the Bible, His infallible Word. Secular psychology is committed to the radically opposite presupposition of humanism, a doctrine which fervently insists that man is the highest being, the central event in all history. Everything revolves around man and is evaluated in terms of its advantages to man. The question before those of us who want to meaningfully tussle with integration is — what is the relationship between the two circles?

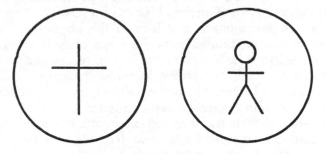

The varying attempts to integrate the circles and thus provide a framework for developing a truly biblical counseling strategy can perhaps be reduced to four distinct approaches.

Separate But Equal

The first might be called Separate But Equal and can be diagrammatically represented as follows:

SEPARATE BUT EQUAL

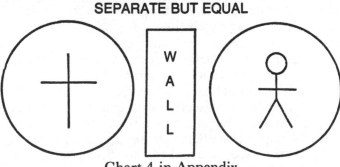

Chart 4 in Appendix

33

Advocates of this position believe that Scripture deals with spiritual and theological problems involving Christian belief and practice. It is felt that many areas of legitimate concern, such as medical, dental, and psychological disorder, fall outside the range of uniquely Christian responsibility and should be dealt with by qualified professionals. Scripture, it is pointed out, was not meant to serve as a medical textbook or as a guide to professional health treatment of any sort, no more than it was intended to be a comprehensive record of ancient history or a scientific treatise. If a person has pneumonia, send him to the physician, not the pastor. If he wants to build a home, have him consult an architect and a contractor. If he has money to invest, recommend a financial consultant. And, continuing in parallel fashion, if he has psychological problems, if he is mentally ill, have the wisdom to refer him to a trained professional counselor.

Pastors with little training and experience in counseling and less inclination for it should refer troubled people to a competent counselor, *but not because psychological problems belong to a sphere unrelated to Christianity.* Many assume that Scripture has no more relevance to emotional problems than it has to pneumonia. The difficulty with this common thinking arises when you look into what we call mental illness. Psychological malfunctions usually consist of or stem from problems like guilt, anxiety, resentment, uncontrolled appetites, lack of self-acceptance, feelings of personal unworthiness, insecurity, wrong priorities, and selfishness. Even the most casual reading of Scripture quickly reveals that it has a great deal to say about these sorts of problems.

Perhaps a detailed understanding of how these problems interact to produce psychological symptoms is something which psychology can help us to understand better. But without question the kinds of problems which constitute the substance of emotional disorders are difficulties to which the Bible speaks. To create a wall between Scripture and psychology and to assume that the two disciplines are Separate But Equal, each dealing with different problem areas, must be rejected firmly as an inaccurate reflection of biblical content.

Tossed Salad

A second approach to integration resembles the strategy followed in preparing a tossed salad: mix several ingredients together into a single bowl to create a tasty blend.

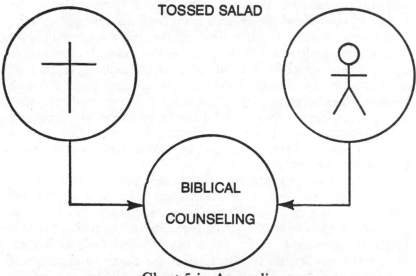

TOSSED SALAD

BIBLICAL

COUNSELING

Chart 5 in Appendix

The weakness of the first approach is corrected by this one. Because Scripture deals with so many of the problems encountered in a counseling office, the counselor who is a Christian will want to add to his therapeutic arsenal a working knowledge of relevant biblical concepts and supporting verses. Quentin Hyder, in his well-received *Christian's Handbook of Psychiatry*, illustrates this sort of thinking. He discusses the value of biblical doctrines such as forgiveness in dealing with the problem of guilt. His thesis seems to be that secular psychological theory has not exhausted the means available for helping people lead productive, whole lives. Christianity, he points out, offers great and at times indispensable resources (e.g., faith, love, hope, trust, purpose) which a knowledgeable Christian therapist can draw upon as needed.

It is my impression that most Christian professionals have adopted this approach to integration: combine the insights and resources of Scripture with the wisdom of psychology and a truly effective and sophisticated Christian psychotherapy will emerge. Christian integrationists tend to align the two disciplines of theology and psychology, determine where the subject matter overlaps, and then blend the insights from both disciplines together. The process is much like bringing together two completed halves of a jigsaw puzzle to finish the picture. For example, hamartiology, the theological study of sin, and psychopathology, the psychological study of mental deviance, both deal from different perspectives with roughly the same subject, human distress. Integration in a Tossed Salad model might be achieved by putting hamartiologists and psychopathologists into a single room to compare notes and arrive at a comprehensive, synthesized view of the human predicament.

The critical problem with the Tossed Salad model is a de-emphasis on the need for a careful screening of every secular concept in the light of Christian presuppositions. Because psychology grows out of a set of presuppositions which are violently antagonistic to Scripture, a model which fails to deliberately scrutinize secular concepts opens the door to a synthesis of contradictory ideas. The Bible assumes that there is absolute truth. Whatever contradicts truth is false. Scripture absolutely refuses to accommodate concepts which are in any way inconsistent with each other. Whenever we mix concepts springing from opposed philosophical positions, we are in danger of moving off our presuppositionary base.

All truth is certainly God's truth. The doctrine of general revelation provides warrant for going beyond the propositional revelation of Scripture into the secular world of scientific study expecting to find true and useable concepts. But we must be careful. Let me explain why, especially when we look to psychology for help. And here I get a bit technical. Psychology deals largely with unobservable or hypothetical constructs. Although ingenious strategies have been designed to measure these unobservable concepts, a strict empirical approach has robbed unseen reality of much of its common sense meaning. Logical positivism and dust bowl empiricism are positions which demand that every meaningful term be defined exhaustively in terms of an empirical, observable referent. In other words, nothing is meaningful unless we can see it. These approaches to knowledge have been exposed as sterile. More and more people in the scientific community are recognizing that we cannot reduce words like love or soul or beauty to a tangible reality. Important reality often is unseen. A discipline which limits itself to the study of those realities which can be palpably discerned with our five senses will quickly become a precise investigation of trivia.

Psychology, in order to be relevant to the real concerns of people, had to move beyond strict empiricism and to deal with concepts which cannot be measured directly. *As soon as psychology began to do more than report observable data, its conclusions necessarily required a great deal of subjective interpretation.* What we gratuitously refer to as the truths or findings of psychology are really a mixture of data and personal interpretation. Now here is the point. Interpretation reflects presuppositions. Psychology's findings typically represent *interpreted data* and therefore reflect to some degree a wrong set of presuppositions. It is impossible for the discipline of psychology to remain metaphysically neutral and purely descriptive when it deals with unobservables. We must therefore move with extreme caution in accepting the conclusions of secular psychology into our Christian thinking. We may be absorbing ideas which subtly contradict our biblical position. Again, let me insist that psychology does offer real help to the Christian endeavoring to understand and solve personal problems. However, the first priority of responsible integration efforts is to develop a strategy for evaluating secular psychology in the light of Scripture.

Buswell puts it well when he says that the person and work of Christ is " . . . the central truth of the entire system of truth and reality in the universe, the truth so integrated with all other truth as to sustain it and be revealed in it."[2] Integration then becomes a

37

matter of determining which psychological concepts flow gracefully from the central Christian presuppositions. We must do more than mix a tossed salad by matching concepts from two disciplines into a synthesis which allows each concept to retain fidelity to its own presupposition. The Tossed Salad model, although often practiced unwittingly by Christians who hold a high view of Scripture, can result in thinking which subtly moves us away from Christianity into sheer humanism.

Let me illustrate how a Tossed Salad approach can get you in trouble with Christian truth. Transactional Analysis offers a neat, simple theory of personality and interpersonal dynamics which has gained widespread popularity in many evangelical circles. Its basic teaching, that people who hold negative convictions about themselves usually develop problems, is perfectly acceptable to Christians. The clear, easily understood division of personality into three parts (Parent, Adult, Child) roughly corresponds to biblical descriptions of conscience (Parent), self (Adult), and sin nature (Child). Transactional Analysis basically involves a study of the interpersonal encounters or transactions to determine which part of the personality was engaged in any given interchange. Counseling then becomes a matter of helping people to recognize when their behavior springs from an overbearing conscience (Parent) or from a selfish childishness (Child) and encouraging the deliberate effort to respond maturely, realistically, and reasonably, like adults.

Nothing said so far is offensive to Christians. We should behave maturely rather than tyrannically or childishly. Because the system is relatively easy to understand and because of its apparent compatibility with Christian thinking, some have embraced T.A. as a useful model for Christian counseling. But there are problems. Listen to the assumptions specified as underlying T.A. in the popular book *I'm OK — You're OK* by Tom Harris.

1. God is an impersonal force (Harris accepts Tillichian theology).

38

2. Man is basically good. Sin is nothing more than the unfortunate, learned conviction that "I am not OK." There is no room in T.A. for objective, moral guilt.

3. Redemption is the process of discovering that my painfully negative self-assessment is not and never has been true. I am really OK, acceptable exactly as I am. The position parallels universalism with its teaching that all people are OK although some suffer under the fear that they are not.

4. Man is sufficient for himself.

My concern is that the theory of T.A. reflects the presuppositions of T.A. An uncritical acceptance of T.A. concepts and practices into Christian counseling can have devastating effects. Sin is never discussed. It isn't part of the system. Faith as the basic means of appropriating divine resources is irrelevant because we don't need supernatural help. Issues of morality are obscured by (1) an insistence on reasonable adult behavior, (2) including sin as part of our childishness, and (3) treating material from our conscience (Parent) as suspect. Putting off the old man is reduced to disengaging the Child or Parent. Putting on the new man is redefined as Adult responding. The idea that people can choose to behave acceptably in their own strength does not reflect and is horribly inconsistent with the revelation of Jesus Christ. The work of the Spirit in motivating and enabling transformation, the efficacy of the atonement in providing the new life, and dependence upon the Word in guiding our changes are all neglected.

When systems are blended together without definite concern for their differing presuppositions, one system will over time "eat up" the other. If a counselor integrated T.A. procedures into his work without extreme care, Christian content could soon disappear or perhaps remain as a useful adjunct. The central problem with Tossed Salad integration is not that secular psychology has nothing to offer, but rather that a careless acceptance of secular ideas may lead to an unplanned compromise with biblical doctrine. Integration is not primarily a matter of aligning theology with relevant psychology. The first job of the integrationist is to screen secular concepts through the filter of Scripture; then we can align those concepts which pass through with appropriate theological matter and attempt to assimilate them into a comprehensive whole. The Tossed Salad model fails to emphasize enough the critical and prior job of screening.

Nothing Buttery

A third approach to integration appears to be a well-motivated overreaction to the first two. Separate But Equal fails to recognize the relevance of Scripture to psychological problems. Tossed Salad adds scriptural concepts to psychological thinking rather than begin with Scripture and cautiously scrutinize psychological concepts in the light of biblical presuppositions. Nothing Butterists (and this includes both theologians and psychologists) neatly handle the problem of integration by disregarding psychology altogether. Their basic tenet is Nothing But Grace, Nothing But Christ, Nothing But Faith, Nothing But the Word. This approach can be sketched easily.

NOTHING BUTTERY

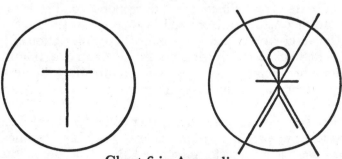

Chart 6 in Appendix

Let me respond briefly to this position before I discuss it more thoroughly. I too believe in the sufficiency of Christ for every need of man, but I don't believe we are denying His sufficiency when we accept secular thinking which in no way contradicts the revelation of Christ in His Word. In Buswell's language, concepts

40

are acceptable if Christ sustains them and is revealed in them. Using concepts which pass this test does not contradict the truth that Jesus is all we need nor does it rob our Lord of His preeminent position.

The philosophy behind Nothing Buttery seems to include a number of ideas, many of which correct the errors implicit in the first two approaches.

1. Scripture does not pretend to offer detailed guidance on external physical issues (curing pneumonia, building a house, etc.). As long as we carefully remain within broad biblical principles, we may validly turn to medicine, engineering, architecture and other "secular" disciplines for the assistance they offer without compromising our Christian position.

2. Everything we need to know to live effectively is included in Scripture, either directly and specifically through teaching or indirectly and generally through example. The personal problems which plague so many (not including problems caused by physical disorder) always stem from sin, simply defined as a failure to follow God's principles for living, a missing the mark of God's intentions and standards. Nothing Butterists insist that psychological disorder is best understood and approached as a set of problems caused directly by sinful or unbiblical living. With psychological notables like Thomas Szasz and O. Hobart Mowrer they firmly reject the assumption implicit in much of our thinking that mental illness represents a foreign invasion of mental germs or an assault from a battering early childhood which has debilitated or warped our internal psychic structures.

3. Since the Bible includes God's revelation of how He deals with sin and a comprehensive statement of godly principles for living, a counselor needs to know *Nothing But* Scripture in order to deal effectively with *every* non-organically caused problem.

4. A major emphasis among Nothing Butterists is that

41

people are responsible for their behavior. They go on to stress that psychological problems are caused *not* by what happens to you but rather by how you respond to whatever happens. And people are responsible for (and by implication capable of) responding biblically to every situation.

5. In the light of these concepts, counseling essentially involves two steps: (1) identification of the sinful pattern assumed to underlie whatever surface problem exists and (2) exhortation and guidance to deal with the pattern by confession (putting off the old man) and a definite repentance reflected in changed behavior (putting on the new man).

In my judgment Nothing Buttery has a great deal to commend itself to the committed Christian. In the sometimes secular world of what passes for Christian psychology, it is refreshing to hear such a strong insistence on the authority and centrality of Scripture. Emphasis on personal responsibility is welcome relief from those who excuse sinful behavior as unfortunate symptoms of mental disease. I read somewhere that Richard Speck's psychologist explained Speck's cold-blooded murder of eight nurses as a "psychological necessity." Skinner would have us blame environments. Freud points the accusing finger at internal psychic disturbance. Rogers empathizes with a stifled person denied his right to self-expression. In every case the person as a responsible agent is lost. Responsibility is gone and, in the minds of many a welcome corollary, so too is guilt. Eliminate responsibility and you do away with guilt. Do away with guilt and sin no longer exists. With the removal of sin the cross of Christ becomes a religious martyrdom rather than the basis of redemption. Score another plus for Satan. Nothing Butterists return us to responsibility, guilt, sin, and the atoning work of Christ. For that we gladly thank them.

At this stage in my thinking I take issue with my Nothing Butterist colleagues primarily on two grounds: (1) their insistence that psychology has nothing to offer and (2) what counseling in

42

their model so easily reduces to — identify sin and command change. The implication is that counseling is no more complicated than finding wrong behaviors, instructing people on *what* they should do differently, and planning, exhorting, and demanding appropriate changes.

The first point has been dealt with already in my discussion of the Tossed Salad model. I stated there that we had to be careful in accepting psychological findings into our thinking and tactics. But I hope I made it clear that if we do screen secular psychology, we will find some ideas (perhaps many) that are consistent with Scripture and do, in fact, add to our understanding of human functioning. For example, Adam, in Genesis 3, dealt with his sin problem by rationalization and projection; he excused his behavior (rationalization) by blaming Eve (projection). He really deceived himself by denying personal responsibility for sin. Jeremiah tells us that all of us are by nature prone to self-deception ("The heart is deceitful above all things, and desperately wicked: who can know it?" Jer. 17:9). Certainly a Christian psychologist would want to study this characteristic of self-deception and would want to understand the many specific ways in which we practice it. Anna Freud, Sigmund's daughter, has written a classic work on ego-defense mechanisms, strategies designed to help us avoid facing unpleasant realities about ourselves. She has observed a variety of ways in which people practice self-deception. Her writings therefore are appropriate and helpful reading for a Christian. More will be said in a moment about the valid use of secular psychology when I discuss the fourth approach to integration.

The second aspect of Nothing Buttery which concerns me is what I think is a simplistic model of counseling. Is counseling nothing more than listening until you detect a sinful pattern of behavior and then pouncing on it authoritatively, instructing people to conform to biblical patterns? As I look into my own life, the fundamental dynamic behind whatever spiritual growth has occurred has been a profound sense of God's unconditional love and acceptance, made possible through Christ's atoning work on

43

the cross. When I experience the inexpressible thrill of *acceptance*, I am motivated to love God in worship and service. Counseling which claims to be Christian must contradict neither the character of God nor the efficacy of the cross. God is holy, righteous, and just. All His anger and wrath have been poured out on Jesus, when He endured the punishment my sins deserved. As one writer put it, "He has drained the last dark drops of the cup of God's wrath; there's nothing but love left for me." Because I am justified, I will never experientially know the wrath of a holy God. Because of the cross, I now am slowly exploring the infinite reaches of His love. Throughout all eternity I will never find the limits of His love. There are none.

Because it is so hard for people to lay hold of total acceptability in Christ, counseling must at every point reflect God's acceptance of the justified sinner. Rebuke and confrontation have a real and often necessary place in counseling but must always occur in the context of true acceptance. A model which emphasizes exhortation and correction can easily neglect the critical dynamic of acceptance. Without establishing a rapport and relationship in which genuine acceptance is communicated, authoritarian correction will produce either rebellion or pressured conformity. Neither promotes spiritual maturity.

A related problem with the simplistic model of "identify, then exhort" is its mechanistic flavor. Carl Rogers has impressively documented in hundreds of hours of counseling that relationship variables are tremendously powerful in effecting improved functioning. People are social beings. We were made that way by God. Counseling needs to take into account the strong influence of interpersonal dynamics. To downplay the relationship between counselor and client in favor of an information-giving model (as Nothing Butterists tend to do) is to reduce personal encounter to mechanistic interaction. Fixing a car requires no more than an understanding of the principles of engine functioning and the like and then doing to the car whatever needs to be done to make it conform to those principles. "Fixing" a person is quite different. In addition to a knowledge of principles of effective living, a deep, genuine concern for the individual *must* be communicated if real character growth is to be achieved.

Another questionable corollary to the simplistic counseling model is the insistence of Nothing Butterists that all personal problems result from sin. In one sense, of course, this is unarguably true. There would be no problems of any sort in all of God's creation if sin had not worked its corrupting effect. Nothing Butterists seem to go a big step further and insist that definite personal sin is immediately responsible for whatever problem a person is experiencing. Although such thinking is attractive to those of us who are tired of excusing sinful behavior as uncontrollable reactions to mental illness, the model cannot always be directly implemented in the real world.

Think of the child who from his earliest days has been either beaten or neglected depending on the mood of his alcoholic father. For years he has been subjected to a world where there is nothing but pain. At age sixteen he is sent to a psychologist by a welfare worker. He is unresponsive, withdrawn, and barely performs essential functions of eating and elimination. Sometimes he sits motionless for hours. A secular therapist labels him catatonic schizophrenic and treats him with drug therapy, following the Freudian notion that ego-less psychotic patients are poor candidates for psychotherapy. If the therapist were behaviorally oriented, he might develop a contingency management program of reinforcing appropriate behaviors with money, candy, or tokens which can buy other things the boy might want. Hopefully the association of love and attention with the more primary reinforcers would create a desire for relationship variables which then could be used to further his progress.

Suppose a Christian counselor with Nothing Butterist leanings were assigned to his case. With his rallying cry ringing in his ears, "There is no such thing as mental illness, only sinful patterns of living," would he quickly attack the many wrong patterns which comprise the boy's entire life style? Exactly where does the issue of personal sin fit? Certainly the patient is exercising no faith in a sovereign, loving God; he is bearing no fruit for the Lord but is

45

rather cowering in a corner, controlled not by the Holy Spirit but by fear. But what do you actually do? Identify sin and command change?

The undeveloped person hiding beneath the layers of defensive withdrawal would retreat further into himself if he perceived the therapist critically confronting him with his sinful responses to an unfortunate set of circumstances. His primary need is acceptance. Would it not be better to provide a new world of love, attempting to communicate real acceptance in some way that would get through? Perhaps a behavior therapy program would be useful to establish contact, an avenue for communication. Drugs might help to reduce anxiety or, if needed, to activate a shut-down nervous system. In some cases active confrontation *might* be the best way to convey respect for the person as a worthwhile individual capable of responding in appropriate ways. Insisting on low-level change often is an effective therapeutic maneuver. Whatever the strategy, the immediate goal is to create an atmosphere of acceptance, a new world into which the boy will risk poking his head. At some point an insistence that he respond appropriately would be in order but not until the child had been given reason to believe that someone out there in the real world cared.

Let me summarize my thinking on this point. Many of the people we deal with in counseling are hiding behind all sorts of defensive overlays designed to protect a fragile sense of self-acceptance or to prevent further rejection or failure from reaching an already crippled self-identity. Counseling involves a stripping away of the layers, sometimes gently, sometimes forcefully, to reach the real person underneath. The context of all such efforts must be genuine acceptance or, as Rogers puts it, unconditional positive regard for the worth of the individual. When the person inside is reached, the truths of Scripture need to be presented in a way suited to the individual's condition. To paraphrase Paul in 1 Thessalonians 5:14, if he is rebellious and willfully wrong, confront and rebuke; if he is weak, scared, insecure but trying, provide whatever strength and assistance you can. (The resources of a local body should be especially valuable in such cases.) With everyone, regardless of his or her state, be patient and warmly accepting.

To assert that counseling is simply a matter of finding sin and exhorting change conveys a simplistic approach which fails to reflect the essential dynamic of Christianity and which does not fit the realistic demands of counseling situations. The thoroughly qualified biblical counselor is one who draws upon true knowledge wherever he can find it and one who knows how to approach the unique individual before him to reach him with that truth. I therefore question Nothing Buttery in two areas: (1) it discredits all knowledge from secular sources as tainted and unneeded and (2) it tends to reduce the complex interaction of two persons to a simplistic "identify-confront-change" model.

Spoiling the Egyptians

There is a fourth approach to integration which in my mind strikes a needed balance between the unintended carelessness of Tossed Salad and the overreaction of Nothing Buttery. Tossed Salad correctly assumes that secular psychology has something to offer but does not pay enough attention to a possible mingling of contradictory presuppositions. Nothing Butterists appropriately demand that every bit of Christian counseling be thoroughly consistent with biblical revelation but throw out all psychology, including those elements which are (perhaps accidentally) consistent with Scripture.

The model I am proposing might be labeled Spoiling the Egyptians. When Moses led the children of Israel out of Egyptian bondage, he took freely of the goods of the Egyptians to sustain God's people on their journey to the Promised Land. God not only approved of this "spoiling" (taking from), but also planned for it to happen and intervened to make it happen. Now there were some things the Israelites took with them which they should have left behind. Exodus 12:38 speaks of a "mixed multitude" that went up with the Israelites. This group of people apparently held to a different set of values than the Israelites (they denied the

47

Christian presupposition of one true God by still clinging to the false gods of Egypt) but wanted to get in on expected blessing. Their approach parallels the modern version of Christianity which demands no commitment to Christ as Lord but encourages an attitude of "Get what you can from Jesus — He'll make you feel good." One writer has called this a Santa Claus theology. "I'm not particularly interested in your Santa but I sure like what He can give me."

Scripture records that it was this uncommitted mixed multitude which first complained about its lack of provisions in the wilderness and provoked the Israelites to rebellion. The rebellion became such an entrenched pattern that every Israelite except two (Joshua and Caleb) acted like unbelieving pagans and died in the wilderness. Spoiling the Egyptians is therefore a delicate and risky task, appropriate for the Christian and sanctioned by God but by no means free of real danger. As I mentioned in the discussion on Tossed Salad, when we mix concepts which are based upon antagonistic presuppositions, one system will "eat up" the other until no Christian content is left and Christian psychology dies in the wilderness, never reaching the Promised Land. But we can profit from secular psychology if we carefully screen our concepts to determine their compatability with Christian presuppositions.

The job of careful screening is no easy matter. In spite of the best of intentions to remain biblical, it is frighteningly easy to admit concepts into our thinking which compromise biblical content. Because psychologists have spent up to nine years studying psychology in school and are pressed to spend much of their reading time in their field in order to stay current, it is inevitable that we develop a certain "mind-set." The all-too-common but disastrous result is that we tend to look at Scripture through the eyeglasses of psychology when the critical need is to look at psychology through the glasses of Scripture.

In recent years a few psychologists who are members of Christian psychology organizations have openly suggested that we interpret Scripture in the light of psychology. One man has

48

gone so far as to reinterpret the gospel accounts of demonic activity in psychological terms, insisting that psychologists must adhere to modern empirical research rather than to the culturally conditioned assumptions reflected in the Bible. In contrast, McQuilkin has well stated that " . . . if the hermeneutics of Scripture, the basis of interpreting Scripture, is from the perspective of cultural anthropology or naturalistic psychology, Scripture is no longer the final authority. Cultural relativism, environmental determinism and other anti-Biblical concepts will seep in and gradually take control."[3]

I am aware that efforts to Spoil the Egyptians could easily degenerate into nothing more than another biblical-sounding Tossed Salad in which essential content of Scripture is unwittingly compromised. In order to minimize that possibility, I would like to propose that anyone who wants to work toward a truly evangelical integration of Christianity and psychology should meet the following qualifications.

1. He will agree that psychology must come under the authority of Scripture. McQuilkin defines this concept as follows: "By 'under the authority' I mean that when the teaching of Scripture conflicts with any other idea, the teaching of Scripture will be accepted as truth and the other idea will not be accepted as truth."[4] I might add that the other idea, *regardless of its support from empirical research,* will not be accepted as truth.

2. He must fervently insist that the Bible is God's infallible, inspired, inerrant revelation in propositional form. No one who argues with this doctrine should, in my mind, call himself evangelical.

3. He must agree that Scripture is to have "functional control" over his thinking. Again, I quote from McQuilkin's provocative article: "By 'functional control' I mean that the principles of Biblical priority over contrary non-Biblical opinion is not merely a doctrine to which one swears allegiance but is actually put into practice thoroughly and

consistently."[5] The functional control of Scripture will be less apparent in fields like architecture and engineering, about which Scripture speaks little, and much more critical and obvious in the discipline of psychology, because its subject matter overlaps greatly with biblical content.

4. In order to achieve such functional control of Scripture over an approach to psychology, integrationists must evidence serious interest in the content of Scripture by:

a. At least as much time spent in the study of the Bible as in the study of psychology.

b. Bible study shall be regular and systematic resulting in

c. a general grasp of the structure and overall content of Scripture and a

d. working knowledge of basic Bible doctrine.

e. Opportunity to profit from the Spirit's gifts by regular fellowship in a Bible-believing local church.

Let me now discuss the model I advocate. In diagram form, Spoiling the Egyptians might look like this.

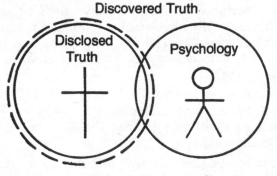

Chart 7 in Appendix

The dotted circle around the circle of revealed or disclosed truth includes all natural or discovered data which is true by nature of

its consistency with revelation.[6] Notice that the circle of psychology overlaps slightly with the solid circle of disclosed truth. In
reviewing the positions of a number of secular theorists, it occurred to me that each theory centered on a principle of human
behavior taught in Scripture. In the appendix to this chapter I
have written nine biblical principles with a brief description of
each. I then listed a few major books by secularists which build on
that principle and develop it in ways useful to a Christian. A word
of caution is added about possible interpretations of the concept
which derive from unbiblical presuppositions.

Some portion of psychology offers ideas and concepts (or,
as I earlier described them, "interpreted data") which do not
contradict the Christian position. In the diagram this is represented by the part of psychology's circle which overlaps with the
larger dotted circle of discovered truth. The books that I list in the
appendix contain some information which would fall in this category. Because of wrong presuppositions however, much of their
thinking runs counter to Christianity and must be rejected. Erich
Fromm offers a useful discussion of love in his book, *The Art of
Loving.* The principle he bases his thinking upon is biblical: people
need love. Some of his insights are helpful like his thought that
love is not defined in terms of its object but rather by a faculty
which enables one to love. But he is far off target in his understanding of the love of God. Since God for him is an impersonal
pantheistic source of energy, one can learn to truly love others by
drawing upon resources already resident in human nature. His
emphasis that people need love is a part of disclosed truth. Some
of his thinking would fall in the overlap between psychology and
discovered truth. Much of his thinking, however, is inconsistent
with Scripture and must be regarded as outside the circle of
discovered truth and therefore unworthy of a Christian's attention.

Another way of stating the matter is to say that psychologists
have discovered useful insights but sometimes use them according
to wrong assumptions. Albert Ellis, psychologist and proclaimed
atheist, has observed that the sentences a person tells himself have

51

a great deal to do with how he thinks and feels. This idea is consistent with Scripture's emphasis on changing your mind in order to act differently (see Rom. 12:1). In one of his articles Ellis proposes that fear of death (an unpleasant emotion) can be reduced by convincing a person that there is no life after death. As the sentence is consciously repeated, "There is no after life, therefore there is no uncertain and potentially painful future to dread," his emotion of fear would subside. The way he uses the biblical principle that "mind influences feelings" is obviously unscriptural. In spite of the wrong ways he uses his idea, his writings helpfully elaborate a biblical principle.

A Christian who has spoiled the Egyptians of secular psychology, carefully weeding out the elements which oppose his commitment to the revelation of Scripture, will be better equipped to counsel than either the Tossed Salad counselor who mixes concepts as they seem called for or the Nothing Butterist counselor who refuses to benefit from the insights of secular study.

Appendix

(1) *Responsibility for Behavior* (Acts 5:1-11).

A. Concept: People should be held responsible for what they do and not blame their sinful behavior on mental illness.

B. Authors:
Menninger — *Whatever Became of Sin?*
Mowrer — *The Crisis in Psychiatry and Religion*
Glasser — *Reality Therapy*

C. Caution: Sin is defined as social offense or irresponsibility.

(2) *Thinking Influences Our Behavior and Feelings* (Rom. 12:2)

A. Concept: What we fill our minds with at any given moment will strongly influence how we feel and what we do.

B. Authors:
Lazarus — *Behavior Therapy and Beyond*
Ellis and Harper — *A Guide to Rational Living*
Maltz — *Psycho-Cybernetics*

52

C. Caution: Proper content of thinking should be determined by Scripture, but in these books it is not. What Ellis calls "rational belief" includes atheism. If you think "no God," you feel no guilt.

(3) *Need for Meaning and Hope* (Acts 17:22-34)

A. Concept: Man cannot function effectively without regarding his present activity as truly significant and meaningful and his future condition as desirable.

B. Authors:

Frankl — *Man's Search for Meaning*

Sartre — summarized in Francis Schaeffer, *The God Who Is There*

C. Caution: Meaning is artificially created rather than tied in to service for God; hope is unfounded optimism or, in absence of optimism, a jump into whatever *feels* good to avoid despair.

(4) *Need for Love and Social Relationship* (Rom. 8:35-39)

A. Concept: Man can function effectively only when he has social relationships; he therefore depends on them and his behavior is understandable only in terms of its social context.

B. Authors:

Adler — *Superiority and Social Interest*

Sullivan — *The Interpersonal Theory of Psychiatry*

Fromm — *The Art of Loving*

C. Caution: Inadequate definition of love; no tie-in to source of love, God; no moral context, no biblical guidelines; no basis for true community (i.e., the body of Christ).

(5) *Most Things We Do Move Toward a Goal* (Matt. 11:28)

A. Concept: People choose to do what they perceive will meet their needs. All our behavior is governed by these choices. Wrong choices depend upon wrong perceptions or beliefs. Paul was willing to live ("For me to live is Christ") and quite

53

willing to die ("to die is gain"). He pressed forward to the goal which God had set before him — conformity to the image of Christ — believing that that goal was indeed the most rewarding. To understand behavior, identify its goal — ask "not whence, but whither."

B. Authors:
Adler — *Superiority and Social Interest*
Dreikurs — *Logical Consequences*

C. Caution: Appropriate goal is never described as maturity in Christ. Adlerians help their patients move in whatever direction the therapist and patient agree is sensible, usually involving elements of humanistic social interest and groundless self-acceptance.

(6) *How We Function in Groups Usually Is Based on Our (Unmet) Needs for Acceptance* (Gal. 2:11-13)

A. Concept: We need to accept ourselves. Most of us don't. Much of our social behavior is determined by our feelings of unacceptability, our resentment at others for not accepting us, our jealousy of others who have what we want, and our desire to get others to accept us.

B. Authors:
Berne — *Games People Play*
Harris — *I'm OK — You're OK*
Rogers — *On Becoming a Person* and *Carl Rogers on Encounter Groups*

C. Caution: Wrong basis for acceptability.

(7) *People Basically Are Out for Themselves But Hate to Admit That to Themselves or Others* (Jer. 17:5-10, especially verse 9)

A. Concept: People essentially are motivated by a desire for self-gratification. Non-believers and "carnal" Christians are characterized by self-interest. Few admit it. Many Christians disguise living for themselves with religious phrases. Ways to hide the truth of your motives from yourself are dealt with in the following books.

54

B. Authors:
Brenner — *Freud, An Elementary Textbook of Psychoanalysis*
Fine — *Freud: A Critical Re-evaluation of His Theories* (Adequately summarizes basic analytical views and the important concept of defense mechanism.)

C. Caution: These authors hold that problems can be solved by living for yourself in a socially acceptable manner.

(8) *Personal Authenticity: Be Who You Are* (Rom. 12:6)

A. Concept: There is real need for honesty with yourself, an open awareness of your feelings, and a non-phony expression of the real you.

B. Authors:
Jourard — *The Transparent Self*
Perls — *Gestalt Therapy Verbatim*
Rogers — *On Becoming a Person*
Coulson — *Groups, Gimmicks, and Instant Gurus* (good summary book)

C. Caution: The "real you" involves a cesspool of feelings, an imagination capable of scheming hideous sins, and a basic motivation of self-centeredness. Scripture teaches that the "new man" in Christ is to find realness in emotion through fellowship, realness in behavior through ministry, and realness in thinking through learning.

(9) *We Are Subject to Environmental Influence* (Gen. 1:28 speaks of dominion over environment. Genesis 1:17-19 suggests that the Fall interfered with man's dominion; now he is partly subject to nature.)

A. Concept: We learn to be afraid of heights by conditioning: we see someone fall on TV, we are told about broken bones, etc.

B. Authors:
Skinner — *Beyond Freedom and Dignity*
Wolpe — *Psychotherapy by Reciprocal Inhibition*

Caution: We are controlled totally by environment. Scripture speaks of new life in Christ which does not enable us to stop weeds from growing in our garden but which does enable us to pull them out without grumbling. Cure for personal problems is not rearrangement of circumstances but realignment with God's Word.

Summary

Man is responsible (Glasser) to believe truth which will result in responsible behavior (Ellis) that will provide him with meaning, hope (Frankl), and love (Fromm) and will serve as a guide (Adler) to effective living with others as a self- and other-accepting person (Harris), who understands himself (Freud), who appropriately expresses himself (Perls), and who knows how to control himself (Skinner).

Notes

[1]A modern approach to counseling discussed more fully later in this chapter.

[2]J. A. Buswell, *A Systematic Theology of the Christian Religion* (Grand Rapids: Zondervan, 1962).

[3]J. Robertson McQuilkin, *The Behavioral Sciences Under the Authority of Scripture.* Paper read at Evangelical Theological Society, December 30, 1975, Jackson, Miss.

[4]*Behavioral Sciences.*

[5]*Behavioral Sciences.*

[6]I am indebted to Donald Tinder for suggesting the terms "disclosed truth" and "discovered truth."

PART II: BASIC CONCEPTS: WHAT DO YOU NEED TO KNOW ABOUT PEOPLE IN ORDER TO EFFECTIVELY COUNSEL?

CHAPTER 3

Personal Needs: What Do People Need to Live Effectively?

I once spoke with Mr. A who had just purchased an expensive home for his family. He was beginning to make a substantial income but had not yet recovered from serious debt. It seemed to me that buying a less expensive home and paying off a few overdue loans would have been a more responsible thing to do. This sort of behavior was one of many such irresponsible actions. I asked him why he bought the large home, looking for an explanation for his irresponsibility. He told me that he loved to invite people over and listen to them admire his home. It made him feel good inside. Why did he feel good? What *need* was Mr. A trying to meet with a fancy house?

Mrs. B felt cold toward her husband and was strongly attracted to another man. She was a Christian woman and felt terribly guilty over her feelings. I asked her how the two men differed. Mrs. B really couldn't list any important differences between the two men except one: she was supposed to be committed to her husband but her relationship with her paramour involved no commitment whatsoever. What *need* was threatened by commitment?

Mr. C told me he was a pathological liar and I believed him. It appeared that his lies always put him in a favorable light with respect to business success. He would tell his wife he had made a bundle that day and wanted to celebrate by going out to a fancy restaurant. The truth was he had just been fired. If friends wanted to do something with him and his wife which he couldn't afford, he would borrow the money, tell his wife he had earned it, and go out for a good time. Why did Mr. C lie? To say that he is a sinner is true, but it does not fully explain his lying. What *need* did Mr. C's lying meet?

A middle-aged woman (Mrs. D) fell into a deep depression after her children left home. Her husband had just accepted a job which took him away from home a great deal. She was now on her own more than she had ever been in her life. Her depression seemed to date back to an important decision she had made on her own which turned out badly. Why was Mrs. D depressed? In order to understand her depression, you must answer another question. What *need* was being protected by Mrs. D's depression?

Deep inside each of these people rumbled a persistent demand, one which they couldn't clearly hear themselves saying, yet one which was driving them ruthlessly in disastrous directions. If we could listen to the faint but powerful murmurings of their unconscious minds, we would hear something like this:

I need to respect myself as a worthwhile person. Sometimes I don't feel like a person at all. I need to feel whole. I must like myself, accept myself. In order to really accept myself, I must be a somebody. I cannot accept myself if I don't matter to anyone or anything. I must be able to regard myself as important; I must matter somewhere; I must see myself as able to do something that is meaningful to someone. But even if I have that, it isn't enough. If I really am to feel like a worthwhile person, I must be loved by another person, loved unconditionally, accepted just as I am without demand or pressure. If I am loved because I behaved well, I am under pressure to keep on behaving well. I know I might not. Therefore I could lose love. I must be loved with an acceptance that I cannot lose no matter what I do.

Sorting through this "stream of unconsciousness," a simple organization emerges: people have one basic personal need which requires two kinds of input for its satisfaction. The most basic need is a sense of personal worth, an acceptance of oneself as a whole, real person. The two required inputs are *significance* (purpose, importance, adequacy for a job, meaningfulness, impact) and *security* (love — unconditional and consistently expressed; permanent acceptance).

I believe that before the Fall Adam and Eve were both significant and secure. From the moment of their creation their needs were fully met in a relationship with God unmarred by sin. Significance and security were attributes or qualities already resident within their personalities, so they never gave them a second thought. When sin ended their innocence and broke their relationship with God, what formerly were attributes now became needs. After the Fall Adam hid from God, fearing His rejection. They both blamed another for their sin, afraid of what God might do. They were now insecure. The earth was cursed and Adam was instructed to work by the sweat of his brow. There was now a struggle between man and nature. Would Adam have the strength to handle the job? He now was wrestling with threatened insignificance.

The need structure of a person might be diagrammed as seen on the next page.

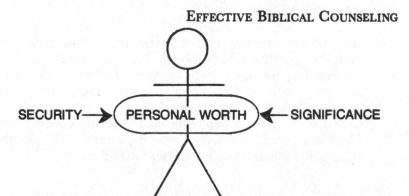

SECURITY—▶ (PERSONAL WORTH) ◀— SIGNIFICANCE

My experience suggests that although men and women need both kinds of input, for men the *primary* route to personal worth is significance and for women the *primary* route is security. Consider the examples at the beginning of this chapter. Mr. A wanted money and the recognition money brings. It is crucial to a proper understanding of him to realize, however, that neither money nor recognition were his ultimate goal. They were merely means to an end. His real goal was significance as a basis for feeling self-worth. He needed to regard himself as significant. And let me insist, at this point, that we must not confuse the sin of pride (I want to run the show, I want my way) with the need for significance. Significance is a normal need, an intrinsic part of man as a personal being, a need which only God Himself can fill, and a need which He wants to fill. Mr. A's problem was not that he needed to be significant. We all do. His real problem was rather a *wrong belief* about what would make him significant. He had fallen for the devilish American myth that money and prestige make you into a someone and he had totally rejected the Lord's teaching that in order to find yourself (to be truly significant and hence a worthwhile being), you have to lose yourself in total submission to the purpose of God in your life.

Mrs. B's problem was due partly to threatened significance, but was more basically related to a deep fear of rejection. Her need for security was involved. A committed relationship required a maturity she had never developed. As a youngster she had been pampered to the point where she came to believe that love was a one-way street. All you had to do was sweetly make your needs known. If there was no response, cry, sulk, or charmingly smile and a loving benefactor would appease you by giving in to your every demand. The result of such training was (in Adler's terms) an undeveloped social interest, a felt inability to give. The first year of her marriage was a frolicking good time. Husband and wife were infatuated with each other, they were good looking, healthy, sexually alive, had plenty of money and no in-law problems. But the realities of two separate human beings living together soon caught up with them. It became apparent that lifelong marriage required a mature commitment beyond what the first year's honeymoon demanded. Mrs. B felt threatened. "Can I do it? I've never had to give. Maybe I can't please him. I'm used to being loved without having to do anything. But marital love is a two-way thing and I have to give myself to it."

As we talked it became clear that the few times she received disapproval in childhood were instances where she had failed to meet other people's standards of performance. Although as a child an indulgent love was consistently hers for the asking, she was dimly aware of the possibility of rejection for failing to measure up. Now she was wondering how her husband would react when he saw her as she was, as he looked beneath the pretty face and the fun personality. She was worried that even if she were to commit herself to the marriage and responsibly try to be a good wife, she might prove inadequate for the job (threatened significance need) and therefore be rejected (threatened security need).

A typical human pattern is the tendency to flee to safety when needs are threatened. She knew she could win acceptance in an immature relationship which demanded nothing from her beyond being attractive and fun. A committed relationship in which she had to give of herself as a person and maturely try to satisfy another human being provided an opportunity for her to be rejected. The risk of commitment was overwhelming. She told me that even her adulterous daydreams never included becoming

63

serious with another man. For her it was safe to flit about from one uncommitted relationship to another, never facing the awful possibility that she actually could be rejected by someone. Notice that Mrs. B's dilemma becomes understandable when we discuss her threatened need for security.

Mr. C, the consistent liar, had a problem similar to Mr. A's problem. He believed that significance depended on always being able to live up to a certain image. He was a good-time Charlie, Mr. Friendly, one of the guys. Everyone liked Mr. C except his wife. She knew he was a phony. How did he get this way? Why did he lie so much? Mr. C recalled to me the day when, as a youngster, he wanted to go with the neighborhood circle of friends to the carnival passing through their rural town. But he needed $2.50, which he didn't have. He remembered going from one family member to another, then to neighbors, looking for someone to give him the required money. But no one gave it to him. As he sat in my office, he vividly recalled (and actually experienced) feelings of desperation — it would have been sheer horror for him to admit to the kids he didn't have enough money to go. Although raised in a rigidly moral home, his conscience gave way under the weight of his need to be a someone in the eyes of his peers. He stole the money from a local grocery store. Other background factors, including a father who never provided adequately and a mother who constantly complained about it, taught him an approach to meeting significant needs which produced many problems.

In Mr. C's mind, his deep need for significance could be fulfilled only if he never had to admit financial failure to friends or family. Facing their expected rejection, scorn, and criticism represented an ordeal to be avoided at all cost. Most of his personal problems revolved around this wrong assumption about what he needed and what he must avoid in order to be a someone. In his adult life he always had to go first class in whatever business he initiated. He had to prove his success. Available capital was never sufficient to handle the exorbitant and outlandish expenses he incurred in his pursuit of significance. As a result, successive businesses, each of which probably could have been profit-making, fell one by one into bankruptcy. One psychiatrist had labeled this pattern as a fear of success. I think, rather, it represented a fear of being in a situation where success was expected. Most neurotic behaviors are attempts to provide excuses for lack of success. Mr. C desperately needed financial success to bolster self-esteem, but was terrified of being in a position where he should be able to make money. In that situation he might fail and failure would utterly devastate his sense of personal worth. He therefore created problems (unconsciously) in his business which he could then blame for his lack of success. If he made good money he could claim success in the face of adversity. If he failed he could shift the blame for failure to the problems and away from himself, thus protecting his self-esteem.

Predictably his self-created problems led to repeated business failures. Although pushing responsibility for his business collapses on to his circumstances helped protect his fragile sense of personal worth, the situation left him in the unbearable position of not having enough money to keep up with his friends and provide well for his family. Any question from his wife about financial matters, no matter how innocent ("Can we afford to buy Johnny a new pair of shoes?"), was felt as a criticism and triggered deep hurt and occasional angry outbursts. Without enough money to impress his friends and family, lying became the only means available to maintain some sense of self-esteem. Whenever people probed beneath the lies and pinned him down to the truth, he simply resorted to blaming external problems for his financial crunch. To admit "I have no money and it's my fault" was for him absolutely equivalent to stating that he was a nobody, a being thoroughly devoid of any personal worth or importance.

A typical attitude encountered in an immature personality is, "It's not my fault. I will not admit failure." To admit failure defeats the purpose to which the immature person is passionately dedicated: protect your self-esteem; it's a fragile commodity. His commitment is to avoid commitment, to never really assume responsibility. Always leave yourself a cop-out: "I will do this if

. . . but if such and such happens, I no longer will hold myself responsible." As long as he can avoid responsibility, he can avoid personal failure. Self-acceptance for so many people depends upon performance. What a tragedy in light of the fact that Christ's death provided God with a basis for accepting us in spite of our performance.

Mr. C's entire web of deception was predicated on a wrong assumption: "In order to be significant, I must avoid disrespect and scorn by keeping up financially with the expectations of my peer group and my family." The pressure to perform produced by this kind of thinking is behind many ulcers.

Consider Mrs. D. She had become seriously depressed after the following things happened: children left home, husband took a job which included extensive travel, a major decision which she had to make while her husband was unavailable turned out badly. The last event seemed to precipitate the depression.

Mrs. D had always been a competent, able woman, raised in a loving family where her abilities were recognized and appreciated. Like so many other children she unconsciously assumed that competence and love were somehow related. She married an unusually strong, gently authoritarian sort of man. Over the years of her marriage she came to depend on his leadership to the point where, without realizing it, she lost some confidence in her own ability to handle situations. These feelings never surfaced however, because she felt quite capable of performing competently so long as her husband was there to back her up, counsel her, and untangle whatever problems she might get into.

Her role as mother provided some real satisfaction for her. Although she made the mistakes all parents make, her kids accepted her as part of an effective parental team. She allowed her husband's quiet strength to slowly undermine her confidence in herself as she came to lean more and more on him. When the children left home, she lost a source of acceptance. Her husband then took the new job which kept him on the road for weeks at a time. One morning while he was gone, she woke up feeling tense.

The nervousness increased until she became visibly agitated. Although she tried to ignore it, the feelings continued for a few days. People began to comment on her shakiness and asked her what was wrong.

Apparently the problem was precipitated by a decision required of her on the day her nervousness began. Her basis of security had always been to appear competent and able. Because she never had to be independently competent in her marriage, her confidence in her own abilities had slowly eroded. Now her circumstances demanded a decision she wasn't sure she could make wisely. Her security, which depended on competence and good performance, was threatened. She haltingly made the decision and stumbled on with lingering feelings of anxiety, afraid that at any moment her incompetence would reveal itself and people would be sorely disappointed in her. When the inevitable moment came and she failed in a responsibility, she was face to face with her own worst fears. Because she had always believed that acceptance was conditional on good performance, she was certain no one would accept her, especially her family. When her husband returned, his mild criticism thoroughly devastated her. She fell apart — not because he criticized her, but because she felt utterly worthless and unlovable. "I am acceptable if I perform well. I did not perform well so I am not acceptable. I cannot be loved. I am therefore a worthless human being."

In an effort to protect herself from further blows to her security, she retreated into a motionless depression in which she stubbornly refused to do anything. Her thinking seemed to be: no decisions — no failure; no failure — no rejection; no rejection — no further hurt. Depression was her safety zone. Persistent guilt feelings ("I'm no good; I've hurt people by my wrong decision") not only supported her withdrawal from further possible failures but also served as a subtle means of expressing antagonism toward a world which had hurt her badly. Her self-accusations and derogation became a real burden to her family, especially her husband, who was unable to reassure or comfort her. Adler speaks of the "opponent" in neurosis, suggesting that neurotic symptoms

67

often are directed at someone, perhaps to get attention or to express resentment.

Mrs. D's depression then included two elements: (1) an excuse for avoiding more mistakes and more criticism which would combine to further injure her self-esteem and (2) an expression of hostility at a husband who had unwittingly undermined her self-confidence by his strong, assertive life style. Notice that her personal need was to feel worthwhile based on the security of being accepted by others. Acceptance in her mind was earned by competent behavior. Since her goal of living above criticism by making no mistakes was unreachable, she chose not to live at all. She retreated into total withdrawal. Depression was both the natural result of cutting off all contacts with life and also and more importantly an excuse for no activity. "How can I make decisions when I'm this depressed? I can't do anything. If only I could be freed of this depression, I could function again."

* * *

The point of this chapter is to illustrate and clarify the two basic needs of people. We all need significance and security if we are to function effectively. If we can regard ourselves as significant and secure, we feel worthwhile as persons. Proverbs 18:14 asks the question, "A wounded spirit who can bear?" When a person feels worthless, he will make it a top priority matter to protect himself from an increase in those unbearable feelings and to ease the feelings already there.

Freud initially taught that libidinal needs of power and pleasure were primary and that neurotic symptoms developed when these needs were not gratified. Many counselors today operate on the assumption that when a person's selfish needs for exerting power or experiencing pleasure are not met, he should find some way to satisfy those needs. Counseling often amounts to an effort to help people let go, do their own thing, whatever feels good. "Be yourself, assert yourself, express all that you are" are common expressions in counseling. "Meet your needs for power and pleasure in ways that will not incur society's wrath. Be a socialized self-seeker."

Other counselors look for buried conflicts thwarting the satisfaction of the needs. "What is the trauma lurking in the unconscious which is stifling growth toward the genital personality?" (Freud's term for a maturity characterized by need satisfaction.) Therapy then becomes an exploratory search for hidden problems which, when uncovered, will free the person from his problems. Mental illness is defined as consisting of unresolved unconscious conflicts.

Directive therapists tend to believe that if a person will just behave responsibly, everything will be all right. Counseling becomes little more than the identification of irresponsible patterns of behavior and exhortations to behave responsibly.

My thesis is that problems develop when the basic needs for significance and security are threatened. People pursue irresponsible ways of living as a means of defending against feelings of insignificance and insecurity. In most cases these folks have arrived at a wrong idea as to what constitutes significance and security. And these false beliefs are at the core of their problems. *Wrong patterns of living develop from wrong philosophies of living.* "As [a man] thinketh in his heart, so is he" (Prov. 23:7). When the person's plans to achieve personal worth go awry, he develops symptoms as protection from feeling badly about himself. He will find some way to hide, to cop out, to run away. His neurotic patterns produce genuine emotional pain but he believes it is less painful than the suffering he would have to endure if his protective symptoms were not there and he had to acknowledge fully his own personal worthlessness. Better to hurt badly for other reasons and to maintain some sense of worth (according to a wrong basis for feeling worthwhile) than to be relieved of the suffering neurosis brings and to feel utterly worthless. The choice is between the devil and the deep blue sea. Treatment must include correcting a person's wrong basis for feeling significant and secure and helping him see what is the real route to personal worth. As long as someone believes that he might sacrifice or at least risk his sense of worth by living responsibly, he will choose to live irresponsibly. You will not correct the

69

problem by exhorting responsible behavior. A change in thinking is required.

Many evangelical pulpits compound the problem by doing nothing more than listing the do's and don't's of Christian responsibility. People who are afraid to live responsibly because they might fail are taught to feel guilty for their irresponsible behavior. Biblical teaching must not only insist upon responsible, obedient, Christ-pleasing behavior, but must also include clear explanations of the Christian's basis for significance and security.

In my first book I developed the thought of how a Christian can rightly regard himself as worthwhile. Let me summarize briefly. Significance depends upon understanding who I am in Christ. I will come to feel significant as I have an eternal impact on people around me by ministering to them. If I fail in business, if my wife leaves me, if my church rolls drop, if I work in a menial occupation, if I can afford only a small house and one used car, I can still enjoy the thrilling significance of belonging to the Ruler of the universe, who has a job for me to do. He has equipped me for the job. As I mature by developing Christlike traits, I will enter more and more fully into the significance of belonging to and serving the Lord.

My need for security demands that I be unconditionally loved, accepted and cared for, now and forever. God has seen me at my worst and still loved me to the point of giving His life for me. That kind of love I can never lose. I am completely acceptable to Him regardless of my behavior. I am under no pressure to earn or to keep His love. My acceptability to God depends only on Jesus' acceptability to God and on the fact that Jesus' death was counted as full payment for my sins. Now that I know this love I can relax, secure in the knowledge that the eternal God of creation has pledged to use His infinite power and wisdom to insure my welfare. That's security. Nothing can happen to me that my loving God doesn't allow. I will experience nothing He will not enable me to handle. When problems mount and I feel alone, insecure, and afraid, I am to fill my mind with the security-building truth that at this moment a sovereign, loving, personal, infinite God is absolutely in control. In this knowledge I rest secure.

I might mention in passing that my acceptability in Christ is no warrant for careless living. Scripture also teaches that I am accountable to God for how I live. If I understand accountability, but not acceptability, I will live under pressure to behave well in order to be accepted. If I understand acceptability, but not accountability, I may become casually indifferent to sinful living. When I understand first my acceptability and then my accountability, I will be constrained to please the One who died for me, fearful that I might grieve Him, not wanting to, because I love Him.

True significance and security are available only to the Christian, one who is trusting in Christ's perfect life and substitutionary death as his sole basis of acceptability before a holy God. When the resources of God are not available because of unbelief, the individual is left with no hope for *genuine* significance and security. Life has neither purpose nor unconditional love apart from the Lord. People then develop alternative strategies for learning to feel as worthwhile as they can. Because these strategies can never really work and because they often run up against obstacles, people do not enjoy significance or security, two elements which all of us desperately need if we are to live effective, productive, richly creative, and fulfilled lives.

It intrigues me to observe Freud's conclusion that the two basic drives behind human behavior are power and pleasure or, in his terms, *thanatos* and *eros*. Freud used the word *thanatos,* meaning "death," to refer to the death wish, the final expression of power over nature. *Eros* refers simply to hedonistic pleasure. I wonder if these two drives are not really degenerate forms of the God-created personal needs of significance and security. In a life without God perhaps power and pleasure are all that can be hoped for realistically.

Our world and particularly our country are characterized by two major problems: violence and immorality. Could it be that

71

the inevitable result of a thirst for power is violence? Destroying is the ultimate in power. When pleasure becomes the highest goal, isn't the predictable end product widespread immorality and perversion? God's judgment fell on Sodom and Gomorrah when violence and immorality had reached their peak. The Israelites were sent in to destroy the Canaanites only when the "iniquity of the Amorites was full." God specifically told the Jews that they would conquer Canaan, not because of their own righteousness, but because of the Canaanite's wickedness (Deut. 9:4,5). The land was characterized by violence and immorality. Is this what "full iniquity" means?

In Romans 1:21 Paul states that when people knew God, they refused to glorify Him as God. By not bowing the knee to God's purposes and lordship, they lost all hope of true significance. Paul then adds, "Neither were [they] thankful." Rather than resting in the love of a saving God and living in an attitude of thankfulness for His care and protection, they struck out on their own, thus giving up any real security. The rest of the chapter documents the downward spiral of people who try to make it without God. The end result is violence (backbiting, murder, etc.) and immorality (homosexuality, premarital sex). It is sadly interesting to note the increasing desire for perverted sex in our modern society. Sadomasochism seems to combine the ultimate in degenerated significance and security: total violent power over another person (sadism) and absolute, unresisting, submission to another (masochism). Perhaps my thinking can be clarified with a diagram.

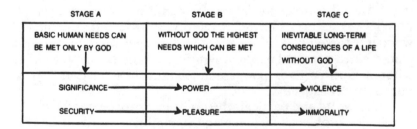

STAGE A	STAGE B	STAGE C
BASIC HUMAN NEEDS CAN BE MET ONLY BY GOD	WITHOUT GOD THE HIGHEST NEEDS WHICH CAN BE MET	INEVITABLE LONG-TERM CONSEQUENCES OF A LIFE WITHOUT GOD
SIGNIFICANCE⟶	⟶POWER⟶	⟶VIOLENCE
SECURITY⟶	⟶PLEASURE⟶	⟶IMMORALITY

Personal Needs

The Christian has all the resources necessary to live in Stage A. When he denies God by swallowing the world's value system (live for money, recognition, fun), he moves over to Stage B where the best he can do is gain power or pleasure. But power and pleasure do not satisfy the basic human need for feeling worthwhile. The Christian can repent and return to true significance and security. Apart from a personal relationship with God through salvation in Christ, no one can move from Stage B to A. The inevitable drift, sometimes over generations but often in an individual's life, is toward Stage C. When Stage C is reached, the stench of sin reaches God's nostrils and provokes Him to judgment. All hope is gone, God "gives them over" (Rom. 1:28) to their own desires as a form of judgment. Hell will be a place where the needs for significance and security will be acutely felt but forever unmet. How utterly horrible. And yet it is the natural consequence of choosing life without God because only in God can our needs be met. Heaven will be a perpetual Stage A, where the need to be worthwhile will continue to be real, but will then be perfectly, at every moment, eternally met by a conscious sense of the significance and security available in relationship to Christ. We will enjoy what Adam experienced before the Fall, but with an important difference: we will not be capable of losing that fellowship. The ground of our perfect relationship with God will not be our innocence but Christ's eternally sufficient atonement. What a hope. Eternal joy. Eternal worth in perfect communion with the One who alone can meet our needs.

CHAPTER 4

Motivation:
Why Do We Do What We Do?

Many people are terribly confused about their own behavior. Why do we do what we do? Paul expressed agonizing bewilderment over his own behavior in Romans 7. He tells us that he regularly found himself doing precisely the opposite of what he honestly felt he wanted to do. As he observed his perplexing pattern of behavior, he could only conclude that there was a law of some sort operating within the structure of his personality which completely opposed his conscious and sincere intentions. Most of us can easily identify with Paul's dilemma.

— A man with a hot temper honestly intends not to lose control again. Within minutes, he's bellowing at his wife, sometimes hitting her. (Wife beating, by the way, is reported to be on the rise, not just in low-income, minority homes, but in middle- and upper-class "respectable" homes as well.)

— Two young people pledge with deeply felt sincerity to love, honor, and mutually care for each other until parted by death. A few years later they lie in bed with their backs to each other, wondering why their marriage is dead.

74

— A wife determines not to let her husband's behavior get her visibly annoyed, but before the evening ends, she has bitingly expressed her irritation.

— After screaming at her child, a mother vows never to raise her voice again. Junior stubbornly refuses to pick up his toys or her teen-age son arrogantly smart-mouths her and her vow is broken with an ear-splitting shout.

— A middle-aged man obsessed with a perverted sexual fantasy feels guilty every time he enjoys his own private world of erotic pleasure. Certain movies and magazines offer such strong temptations that he succumbs. Wrecked by deep remorse, he promises God he will never allow his mind to dwell on his sexual daydreams again. That evening in bed he rehearses in arousing detail another fantasy.

Why? Why, despite our best intentions, do we fail to carry out our sincerely made resolutions? It is not uncommon, when asking this question, to hear any number of completely unhelpful evangelical clichés like, "You're not trusting in the Lord's power, you're depending on your own" or "Let go and let God" or "You're not reckoning your old nature to be dead" or "Pray more earnestly for deliverance, then repeat phrases including 'the blood of Christ' — your problem will disappear." But the problems continue. Many people who conscientiously are trying to change for the better experience serious guilt problems which only compound their difficulties in self-control. What is the answer to the problem? Why do we do what we do even though we consciously may not want to? The answer is not easily expressed in a few words. People looking for a simple, pat answer or an authoritarian, rigid set of principles perhaps will be disappointed in my answer, but I do not believe that anything short of a well-thought-through response will be helpful. In this chapter and the next I want to describe what I believe to be a theory of human motivation which is consistent with a scriptural view of man.

As a starting point let me list five basic propositions about

75

motivation. Read them slowly and carefully. Later discussion will presume knowledge of these principles.

Proposition 1: Motivation typically depends upon a need state, or in simpler language, we are motivated to meet our needs.

Proposition 2: Motivation is a word referring to the energy or force which results in specific behavior. Before it becomes specific behavior, motivational energy is channeled through the mind. It is there that the energy assumes direction. I am motivated to meet a need by doing certain things which *I believe in my mind* will meet that need.

Proposition 3: Motivated behavior always is directed toward a goal. I believe that *something* will meet my need. That something becomes my goal.

Proposition 4: When the goal cannot be reached (or when the individual perceives it cannot be reached), a state of disequilibrium exists (subjectively felt as anxiety). The need which is denied satisfaction becomes a source of negative emotions. In simpler terms, when I cannot have what I think I need to be significant or secure, I feel worthless. I then am motivated to protect my need to feel worthwhile from further injury by minimizing feelings of insignificance or insecurity.

Proposition 5: All behavior is motivated. There is no such thing as an unmotivated person. Laziness, procrastination, withdrawal often are motivated by a desire to protect the self from increased feelings of worthlessness. In analyzing behavior one must never say, "There is no reason for that. It is utterly senseless." All behavior makes sense. It may be sinful, ineffec-

76

> tive, or bizarre, but it does make sense. In order to understand any unit of behavior, you must know what need is motivating the behavior, the person's ideas about what would meet the need, the goal which his thinking has determined as desirable, and the success or failure of the person in reaching the goal.

Let me attempt to clarify these propositions by illustrating how they might explain certain behaviors. I need to feel significant and I am motivated to somehow meet that need (Proposition 1). I have been taught by a false world value system that in order to be important I must have money. I therefore assume that financial wealth makes a person significant (Proposition 2). My goal therefore becomes making as much money as I can (Proposition 3). I listen to the preacher tell me that the love of money is the root of all evil, that I can't serve God and money, that I am supposed to seek first His kingdom and set my sights on laying up heavenly treasures, and that I am to give up my goal of becoming rich. Because I am a Christian and because I believe the Bible is God's inspired Word, I fully agree with what the preacher is telling me, but I still feel an inner drive compulsively spurring me on to make money. I try to shake it but I can't. Prayer, repentance, dedication all make me feel better for a while, but the lust for money remains strong. My real problem is not a love of money but rather a wrong belief, a learned assumption that personal significance depends on having money. *Until that idea is deliberately and consciously rejected, I will always want money*, no matter how many times I confess to God my sin of wanting money.

If I make money, I may feel guilty because I know my desires are wrong, but I will likely feel rather good on the inside. I do attain a measure of significance according to my wrong but firmly held assumption. If I do not make money, I feel worthless (Proposition 4). Perhaps I give up a lucrative job to enter full-time Christian service, but I will not find a sense of real fulfillment until I change my thinking about what makes a person significant. If I continue in my efforts to earn big money, but experience financial reverses, I then may redouble my efforts to rid myself of this consuming desire for money. But again, as long as I unconsciously believe that money equals significance, I never will stop lusting after money because I always will be motivated to meet my needs (Proposition 1). Paul says that transformation depends upon renewing our minds. Said in another way, our motivational energy can be channeled in different directions if we change our thinking about what will meet our needs. My efforts to change should not focus on my behavior but rather on my wrong thinking.

If I don't reach my goal of money and don't correct my thinking, I may resort to unethical strategies to achieve my goal. I will know I'm wrong and will hate myself for behaving sinfully, but I'll do it anyway. Motivation to meet personal needs is overwhelmingly strong. I may develop a seared conscience in order to give myself some sense of peace. Or I may resort to creating a series of maneuvers designed to protect an injured sense of worth (Proposition 4). Perhaps I will develop psychosomatic fatigue, or dizzy spells, or headaches. I might experience psychological problems like depression, anxiety attacks, or insomnia. These problems will serve a useful function in dulling the pain of feeling worthless. I can comfort myself by believing that were it not for this unfortunate problem I likely could become quite successful. My worth is therefore safeguarded in the face of financial failure. Although the symptoms I develop may be neither consciously fabricated nor deliberately intended to serve a useful psychological function, they nevertheless are effective in preventing the worst possible hurt: the conscious admission that I am worthless (Proposition 5). Until I reach that point, any suicide notions I have will be basically manipulative, designed somehow to further protect my sense of worth. When I can no longer avoid the admission that I am worthless, suicide becomes in my mind a rational alternative. (I might mention that either suicidal dynamic can result in a successful suicide.)

78

Motivation

Let me restate the thinking on motivation from a somewhat different perspective. Abraham Maslow's classical need hierarchy suggests that human beings have five basic needs. The lowest one in the hierarchy must be met before the person is motivated to meet the second need and so on up the hierarchy.

The five needs in Maslow's list, starting with the lowest or most basic, are:

1. *Physical* (food, water, etc., elements necessary to maintain physical life).
2. *Security* (Maslow means physical security: some reasonable confidence that physical needs will be met tomorrow).
3. *Love* (what I would call security).
4. *Purpose* (what I would call significance).
5. *Self-actualization* (the expression of the highest qualities of humanness — development of myself into a full, creative, self-expressing person).

The essential feature in Maslow's theory is that people are not motivated to meet the "higher" needs until the "lower" or more basic ones are met. If I have no food right now, I will be less concerned with tomorrow's meal than with today's. If I am deeply worried about dying tomorrow from starvation, I will not be interested in attending a lecture on "Your Purpose in Life." Maslow's listing also suggests (and I tend to agree) that security or love is a more basic need than purpose or significance. However, both are required before I will be motivated to truly express who I am, simply because until I enjoy security and significance, I do not believe I really am anyone.

Since God is an infinite and personal being it follows that man made in His image is a finite and personal being. As a finite being, he is dependent on external resources to meet his needs: he is a contingent being. His needs as a *physical* finite creature correspond to Maslow's first two needs: physical needs met today and the confidence that they will be met tomorrow. Maslow's third and fourth needs (love and purpose) correspond to what I

79

call the *personal* needs of man: security and significance. Self-actualization, the ultimate and highest need in Maslow's system, comes close to the biblical concept of becoming mature in Christ, developing in ourselves those attributes which characterize the Lord and then expressing our God-given worth in freely worshiping God and in serving others by the exercise of our spiritual gifts.

Notice that the first four needs are essentially self-centered. They involve a taking in, rather than a giving out. "I need to draw from outside resources to meet my physical needs and to experience love and purpose." Motivation to meet any of these first four needs might therefore be called *Deficit Motivation,* a desire prompted by a felt lack and designed to supply what is missing. Only the last need of self-actualization allows for a non-egocentric other-centered motivation to give rather than to get. It is interesting to note that Adler measured mental health in terms of the development of what he called "social interest," an active concern with the needs of others. In a similar vein a recent president of the American Psychological Association questioned a model of mental health which stresses self-gratification. He pointed out that our heavy emphasis on individualism has fostered the assumption that freedom from conflict depends upon getting whatever we want when we want it. In his address to a major psychological convention, he suggested that perhaps the important element in human adjustment is not what we get but rather what we give: a concern for the social good as measured by a self-denying responsible adherence to moral standards. This thinking seems consistent with Christ's teaching, "If you want to save your life, lose it."

Now if it is true that mental health is best defined in terms of a person's genuine interest in expressing himself for the good of others, and if it is impossible to reach this stage of self-actualization until the first four egocentric needs are met, then there are some rather startling implications for those of us who take Scripture seriously. In my first book I explain why the personal needs of significance and security can be fully met only in a relationship with a personal God. It therefore follows that only a

80

Christian has the resources necessary to become truly self-actualized. Let me present the argument in logical form.

(1) In order to be well-adjusted, you must reach the stage of self-actualization.

(2) In order to reach that stage you must pass through the other four stages first; your physical and personal needs must be met before you are in a position to become self-actualized.

(3) If *personal* needs can be met only in a relationship with a personal God, *then only a Christian has the resources to reach the fifth stage, to actualize himself, and therefore to be truly well-adjusted.*

Non-Christians may, of course, meet their physical needs at a given moment without consciously relying on the Lord. The need to be assured that physical needs will be met tomorrow can never, in the face of uncertainty of physical and economic well-being, be truly met. But if health is good and if there is plenty of money in the bank, people apparently can go on to be motivated by needs for significance and security. It is at these stages that a non-Christian gets stuck. Without the Lord it is possible to achieve a close facsimile of security in the love of spouse or friends and to feel a definite sense of significance in devoting yourself to a purpose which many would agree is important. On the basis of the counterfeit but subjectively satisfying sources of significance and security, some people do move on to what most observers would agree is a healthy level of becoming self-actualized. But if it is true that every attempt to meet personal needs apart from a committed relationship to Christ must logically fall short of its goal, then every non-Christian must in some sense be forever trapped in Stages 3 and 4. Because he is not and cannot be fully satisfied in his most basic personal needs, there will always be an undercurrent of motivation to find significance and security in all his behavior. He is doomed to egocentricity until he can progress

81

beyond Stages 3 and 4, which he cannot really do without becoming a Christian.

Many non-Christians exhibit a commendable humanitarian interest in other people. Is this not an expression of a truly actualized person? No, because underneath whatever worthy, conscious motivation may exist there must be the demanding rumblings of unsatisfied needs for significance and security. If there are no such rumblings, then it must be possible to become a truly whole person without God. If that is true, hell would be a rather pleasant place where people who found love and meaning without God can enjoy each other. But God *is* utterly indispensable in meeting personal needs. Therefore, no matter how actualized or giving or loving a non-Christian may seem to be, he still is operating from a deficit. The motivational core of his behavior must be stained with a desire to meet his own needs. He still is fundamentally self-centered, prompted by deficit motivation to supply in himself what is missing. God, who sees to the innermost depths of our hearts, cannot commend or accept behavior that is in any way selfishly motivated.

If my reasoning is correct, Christians should be the most self-actualized people around, the most caring and compassionate, most free from egocentricity and the pettiness, squabbling, and sulking resulting from a selfish concern with getting one's own needs met. Theoretically, Christians are in a position to be free from deficit motivation. We could be living consistently beyond Stages 1 through 4 and into Stage 5, using our lives as instruments of God on behalf of others. Yet we often differ not one whit from the self-seeking worldling who is preoccupied with meeting his own needs. Paul rebuked the Christians for living like ordinary men.

The reason for such carnal behavior is not hard to unearth. In a word, the problem is unbelief (or, as I prefer to think of it, wrong beliefs). Sit down with your Bible and find verses which claim that God has promised to meet every need on Maslow's list. What remains for us is to "possess our possessions," to aggressively and persistently believe that He is looking after our needs

82

thoroughly, and to thus live in Stage 5. The Christian is to travel through Stages 1-4 on the wheels of faith. Consider these well-known verses as a basis for your faith. There are, of course, many others.

God has met our physical needs.

"Seek ye first the kingdom of God, and his righteousness; and all these things (referring to food, clothing, shelter) shall be added unto you" (Matt. 6:33).

God has met our need to know that tomorrow our physical needs will be met.

"Take therefore no (anxious) thought for tomorrow" (Matt. 6:34).

"Be [anxious] for nothing; but in every thing . . . let your requests be made known unto God. . . . my God shall supply all your need according to his riches in glory by Christ Jesus" (Phil. 4:6,19).

God has met our need for security (love).

"Who shall separate us from the love of Christ? . . . I am persuaded, that . . . [nothing] shall be able to separate us from the love of God, which is in Christ Jesus" (Rom. 8:35,39).

"God commendeth his love toward us, in that, while we were yet sinners (at our worst, exposed for what we really are, no masks), Christ died for us" (Rom. 5:8).

God has met our need for significance (purpose).

"For me to live is Christ and to die is gain" (Phil. 1:21).

"For we are his workmanship, created in Christ Jesus unto good works, which God hath before ordained that we should walk in them" (Eph. 2:10).

"[God] redeemeth thy life from destruction (squandering, wasting)" (Ps. 103:4).

To the degree that a Christian believes these verses, he is freed from a life of self-centered concern with whether or not his own needs are met, and he is able to move on to real self-actualization, confidently knowing (not necessarily always "feeling") that his physical needs will be met according to God's purposes and that his personal needs are now and forever perfectly met. To believe this in the face of tremendous pressure to agree with the world's false value system of living for money, pleasure, or fame requires a strong commitment to the authority of Scripture. I am distressed to hear some of my colleagues in Christian psychology treat the Bible as helpful but not authoritative. Some seem to regard Scripture as accurate in its teaching on spiritual matters but possibly incorrect in the realm of scientific concerns. Evangelicals, if they are to remain evangelicals in any meaningful sense, must dogmatically insist that wherever Scripture speaks, it speaks with infallible authority. If the Bible says my psychological needs are met, then they are met. Even though my entire personal being may rebel and scream within me, "I feel neither secure nor significant, I am not worthwhile," I must forcibly by an act of my will bow before the Word and admit that somewhere I am not perceiving things accurately. Psychotherapy in its most sophisticated form deals with those inaccurate perceptions and helps a person change them to square with Scripture.

Christians never operate from a deficit, but rather from fullness. Our lives should be an expression of that fullness in worship and service. I therefore refer to the motivation of an appropriately self-actualized person as Expression Motivation. Yet most of us feel a deficit and act in ways designed to fill the void. It is one thing to say that we can claim by faith that our needs are already met in God and therefore live in Stage 5 with Expression Motivation. It is quite another thing to disentangle ourselves successfully from the sticky web of deficit motivation. In the next chapter I will discuss the workings of the human personality in an effort to arrive at a strategy for progressing from deficit to expression motivation and thereby reaching the goal of Christian maturity.

Summary

People are motivated to meet their needs. If they are hungry, they behave in ways designed to secure food. If they are insecure, they try to find love. Until a person's needs are met, he is operating from a deficit. His motivation can be characterized as self-seeking. He is trying to meet his own needs.

Motivation perhaps can best be understood as an energy to do something which the person believes will lead to need gratification. People develop ideas from interaction with a false world system about what is required to meet their personal needs of significance and security. Their beliefs then determine the goals they live for. That goal (whether it be money or power or obedient children or a loving husband) will never be given up until it is recognized that personal needs are met only in a relationship with Christ.

In order to understand why we do what we do, we need to see that most of us operate from deficit motivation, trying to obtain something we believe will meet our personal needs. When the desired goals are not reached, we are motivated to protect ourselves from the painful feelings of insignificance and insecurity. Alcoholism, compulsive spending, overeating, excuse making, many psychosomatic ailments, some forms of schizophrenia[1] and a host of other behaviors often are designed to anesthetize or compensate for the emotional pains of feeling worthless.

Notes

[1]See Paul McReynold's article in *The Etiology of Schizophrenia* by Don Jackson for an excellent discussion of this point.

CHAPTER 5

Personality Structure: Taking Apart the Watch to See What Makes It Tick

In the last chapter I suggested that if we are to understand why we do things we sincerely feel we don't want to do, we must understand that we are motivated to meet our needs for significance and security in ways we unconsciously believe will work. A wife tells me she cannot give herself to her husband sexually. She consciously wants to and tries hard to give him her body in obedience to 1 Corinthians 7:1-5, but becomes so tense she withdraws. Why? Perhaps she believes she needs her husband's love to be secure. Since he has hurt her in the past, she may now be afraid to make herself vulnerable to more hurt by coming close to him. She therefore tightens up and withdraws from sex, the most intimate expression of closeness. Perhaps she also feels some resentment toward him for hurting her and, in addition to not trusting him enough to come close, she withdraws in order to get even.

A counselor who arrives at these conclusions has not yet helped his client. He now must help her change from deficit motivation (behavior with her own unmet needs in mind) to

Personality Structure

expression motivation (behavior which expresses her God-given wholeness in consistency with scriptural direction). If he is going to be able to help her effect this shift and also to successfully handle a wide variety of cases, he will need to understand some basic principles of personal functioning.

In this chapter I want to draw a picture of a person. Artists depict the outside of a person, the external, physical appearance. Anatomy professors sketch the physical insides of a person, showing the bones and organs that lie beneath the skin. I want to go underneath the outer covering too, but rather than trying to detail more of the physical part of persons, I want to try to capture on paper an elusive intangible. Physicians speak of physical anatomy. I am concerned with personal anatomy, the constituent parts that make a person more than a functioning collection of physical parts. I want to draw a *person*. In terms appropriate for a psychologist, I might say that I hope to sketch the psychoanatomy of a person. What are the inside parts of a person? What do we think with? What makes us feel as we do? How do our thoughts, feelings, and chosen behaviors interact?

Before I begin to draw a person, I want to make two important points. (1) I am not what psychologists call a physicalistic reductionist, that is, I do believe that there are intangible "parts" in a person which are not reducible to our physical body. Emotion is more than glandular functioning. Thinking is more than neurological activity in the brain. Although there are intricate connections between physical functioning and personal functioning, I do not believe that how we think, act, and feel as persons can be explained completely in terms of physiological correlates. (2) Whenever we dissect an organism to examine its constituent parts, we are in danger of losing sight of the whole functioning organism. A surgeon may learn to think of the "object" lying on his table as a collection of parts including heart, lungs, liver, brain, and so on. I believe that a person is a functioning entity who acts as a unit. As I discuss the various component parts of this whole person, I may give the impression that I think of a person as nothing more than an assortment of parts. Let me state clearly

87

that I believe a person is an indivisible whole. My effort in this chapter is to better understand how that indivisible whole functions by looking at the key functioning elements within the human personality.

In discussing the parts of a person many Christians begin by talking about the spirit, soul, and body. In my thinking, as I have already implied, it is more useful to think of human beings as composed of two parts: the physical and the personal, or material and non-material. The body belongs to the physical side of man, the spirit and soul to the personal. Although the terms for spirit and soul sometimes are used interchangeably in Scripture, many scholars have attempted to distinguish between them. I tend to agree with the dichotomists who feel that spirit and soul are not separable other than in a functional way. I suggest that the terms can most simply be understood not as reified entities or literal parts of the personality, but rather as descriptive terms which express whether the personality as a whole is oriented primarily toward God or primarily toward other people. When I devote my personal energies toward God in worship, prayer, or meditation, it can be said that my spirit is interacting with God. That is just another way of saying that I as a person am at that moment interacting with God. When I redirect my personality toward another person, when I function laterally as opposed to vertically, I then am engaging my soul with yours.

If spirit and soul really are descriptive terms referring only to the direction of personal functioning, we must concern ourselves with exactly what we mean by personal functioning. The way a human personality works is perhaps best understood by looking at its functioning parts.

The Conscious Mind

The first element in personal functioning is the conscious mind. People have a self-consciousness; we can talk to ourselves in sentences. With this ability to say things to ourselves in propositional form (i.e., we clothe impressions in words), we evaluate our world. When an external event occurs and catches my attention, I respond to it first by talking to myself about it. I may not always notice the sentences I am telling myself, but I am responding in verbal form nevertheless and, if I paid attention to my mind, I could observe what sentences I am using to evaluate this event. For example, if I wake up to a rainstorm on a morning planned for golf, I may mentally evaluate the event with sentences such as, "My golfing partner is a potential client who will be leaving town tomorrow and I perhaps am losing a chance to make big money. This storm is a terrible thing." My emotional reaction would be very negative. If my wife asked me why I felt depressed, I might say, "Because it's raining outside." But that wouldn't be accurate. A rainstorm has no power to make me depressed, but a strong negative mental evaluation of the storm does. In other words, events do not control my feelings. My mental *evaluation* of events (the sentences I tell myself) do affect how I feel. Suppose I were to change my evaluation from "This storm is a terrible thing" to "Money is important but I trust God to meet my needs. Therefore, although I would prefer to play golf today, it is not terrible that I can't." With that sentence in my mind, my emotional reaction would include real disappointment but also a quiet sense of peace.

To those who have studied personality theory, it will be obvious that I am here describing a subjective, phenomenological viewpoint rather than an objective, positivistic one.[1] Freud and Skinner both taught that what *happens to* a person is responsible for his problems. Along with Adler, Ellis, Rogers, and others, I am suggesting that how a person *perceives* what happens to him has a lot to do with his emotional and behavioral reaction. If he perceives what happens as a threat to his personal needs, he will experience strong negative feelings and will deal with the event in a personally defensive manner. Perhaps he will launch an emotional attack on the event trying to change it. (Husbands and wives are specialists in working hard to change each other in order to have their own needs better met.) Or he might withdraw from the event to avoid further hurt. If, however, the event is perceived as personally fulfilling ("in order to be significant, I need recognition; my boss just complimented me on my management ability"), the individual will feel good. If he perceives what happens as irrelevant to his *personal* needs ("Coal miners strike in Britain"), he likely will have no *deep* emotional reaction. How a person mentally *evaluates* an event determines how he *feels* about that event and how he will *behave* in response to it.

The picture I have described thus far can be drawn like this.

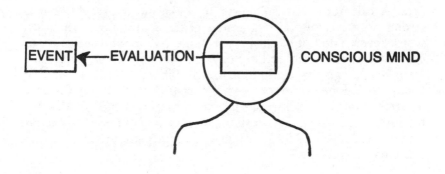

The Greek word translated mind which most closely corresponds to what I have called the conscious mind is *nous*. Vine defines *nous* as " . . . the seat of reflective consciousness, comprising the faculties of perception and understanding and those of feelings, judging, determining."[2] I might define it simply as that part of the person which makes conscious evaluations including moral judgments. Paul uses the word frequently, most notably perhaps in Romans 12:2 where he tells us that transformation into Christlikeness depends on renewing our minds. I take that to mean that my spiritual growth depends directly upon how I perceive and evaluate my world, or in other words, with what sentences I fill my mind in response to a given event. If that is true, it becomes important to know what determines the sentences which I consciously speak to myself in my *nous*. In order to understand why I evaluate events as I do, I have to add another element to my sketch of psycho-anatomy.

The Unconscious Mind

In the Scriptures the Greek word *phronema* sometimes is translated "mind," for example in Romans 8:15. I recently listed every verse in which this word (or a derivative) is used. From my study of these passages, it appears that the central concept expressed by the word is a part of personality which develops and holds on to deep, reflective assumptions. For example, "Those that are after the flesh *mind* the things of the flesh" suggests that people who do not take God into their reckoning are thoroughly infected with the idea that fleshly pursuits lead to personal happiness. Let me tentatively suggest that this concept corresponds closely to what psychologists call the "unconscious mind." Linking these two concepts suggests a definition of the unconscious part of mental functioning as *the reservoir of basic assumptions which people firmly and emotionally hold about how to meet their needs of significance and security.*

Each of us has been programed in his or her unconscious mind to believe that happiness, worth, joy — all the good things of life — depend upon something other than God. Our flesh (that innate disposition to oppose God) has responded happily to the world's false teaching that we are sufficient to ourselves, that we can figure out a way to achieve true personal worth and social harmony without kneeling first at the cross of Christ. Satan has encouraged the development of a belief that we can meet our needs if only we had_____. The blank is filled in differently, depending on one's particular temperament and family and cultural background. An unbelieving world system, energized by Satan and appealing to our fleshly natures, has squeezed us into the mold of assuming that something other than God offers personal reality and fulfillment.

If my father happens to be a professional musician, I may learn the assumption that significance depends upon the development of talent or perhaps upon the recognition of others for performance of a skill. We all develop some *wrong assumption* about how to get our needs met. Adler aptly calls this basic assumption a person's "guiding fiction," an untrue belief which determines much of our behavior and feelings. In the first portion of this chapter I said that the sentences we consciously tell ourselves strongly influence how we feel and what we do. We now can see where these sentences originate. The content of the sentences we tell ourselves in our conscious minds draws upon the wrong assumptions held by our unconscious minds. We often are not aware of our basic wrong belief about how to meet our needs. Yet that ungodly belief determines how we evaluate the things happening to us in our world and that evaluation in turn controls our feelings and behavior. The battle today is for the minds of people. Influence what a person *believes* and you influence the whole person.

To return to my earlier example, if I deeply believe that my significance depends upon a high degree of developed talent, then after I practice the violin for years and still squawk like a beginning student, I likely will evaluate my poor performance (Event) as something very bad *because it is personally threatening*. I then will feel insignificant and either (1) redouble my efforts to master the instrument, (2) develop a safeguarding excuse (e.g., "accidentally" break my wrist) which I can use to protect my worth from further injury by saying, "What a bad piece of luck. Just when I was on the verge of greatness" or (3) retreat into depressed

92

inactivity occasioned by a deep sense of worthlessness and sustained by the safety it provides from further failure.

The picture now looks like this.

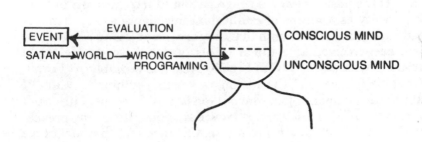

Although the exact form of the wrong programing will vary with each person, there are perhaps a few rather common ideas we are taught to believe, such as:

— "I must be a financial success in order to be significant. Financial worth equals personal worth."
— "I must not be criticized if I am to be secure. Everyone must approve of me in everything I do."
— "Others must recognize my abilities if I am to be significant."
— "My security depends upon my spiritual maturity."
— "My significance depends upon how successful my ministry is."
— "I must not fail (come short of an arbitrarily defined standard of success, usually bordering on perfection) if I am to honestly regard myself as worthwhile."

If our evaluation of events that happen to us depends upon notions like these, it is no wonder that many people are anxious, guilty, or resentful. A woman whose security depends upon absence of criticism will not take kindly to her husband's negative comments about her housekeeping ability. Her resentful feelings at that moment are not a direct response to his criticism but are rather a response to her threatened need for security. If she learned to separate her worth as a person from her husband's approval the same criticism would provoke a much calmer reaction. If the pastor *needs* his congregation to recognize his preaching ability as a means of establishing his significance, then any indication from the church that they are not enjoying his sermons will be perceived as a threat to his personal worth. He might respond with *anxiety* ("Can I really preach acceptably? If I can't, what do I have left? I'm no longer worth anything"), *guilt* ("I always do an inferior job. Maybe God is punishing me. I just can't measure up"), or *resentment* ("How dare you criticize my preaching? You are robbing me of my significance and that makes me angry").

In order to understand why the pastor begins to show nervous mannerisms in the pulpit, or why he glumly loses interest in his work, or why he coolly ignores his critics, you must study his propositional response to criticism, that is, what sentences are running through his conscious mind as he considers the event of criticism. Then you must look for the source of those sentences in an unconsciously held assumption about significance. He has allowed his worth as a person to become wrapped up in his acceptability as a preacher. He has a wrong belief about how to be significant.

For a counselor to explore a person's "assumptive system" (Jerome Frank's term in his excellent book *Persuasion and Healing)* involves shining light on thinking which to this point has been enshrouded in darkness. Counselors must understand that few people welcome unpleasant revelations about themselves. For a man to admit that his business goals represent a thoroughly self-centered ambition to find personal worth is difficult. Wives who for years have been trying to please their husbands and have honestly felt their behavior was giving do not easily acknowledge that in reality they have been manipulating their husbands to be affectionate because they believe that their personal security depends upon their husband's love.

Resistance to owning up to one's selfish guiding fiction takes many forms ranging from outright denial to vague confusion. It is difficult not to become frustrated with a client who responds to everything I say with "Could be, but I don't know — I'm so confused." Nothing is easier than self-deception. Self-discovery is so painful: it wounds our pride and tarnishes the good opinion we cherish of ourselves. Scripture teaches that we are masters of self-deception and that we require supernatural help to see ourselves as we really are (Jer. 17:9,10). Honest and accurate exploration of the inner chambers of one's personal being is the special prerogative of God. Christian counseling at this point depends critically upon the enlightening work of the Holy Spirit. Without His assistance, no one will perceive or accept the truth about his self-centered and wrong approach to life.

Psychologists have long wrestled with the problem of resistance, which may be defined as the effort of the patient to prevent painful unconscious material from becoming conscious. From a psychological point of view, it seems to me that resistance can be explained in two ways. First, an idea which has been strongly reinforced and acted upon for years will yield to change grudgingly. The belief has been a part of the person for so long that it feels comfortable, like a pair of well-worn shoes. Any change from a familiar position, even though the position may be painful, is threatening.

Second, it is important to realize that basic assumptions are more than merely logically held beliefs. If, with our conscious mind, we entertain evaluative propositions, then with our unconscious minds we hold attitudes. Attitudes have affective (emotional) as well as cognitive components. They are developed in the emotionally charged atmosphere of a person's earnest and consuming desire to meet his needs. "I must become worthwhile. How do I do it?" The world then teaches the emotionally starving person what he needs. When he accepts a certain belief and adopts a strategy to establish his worth, he will hold on to his wrong belief with a fierce intensity. To undermine his belief is to cut his lifeline. Counseling which attempts to logically teach new truth without concern for the emotional threat involved in changing one's approach to meeting personal needs will plow headlong into resistance. Again let me underline the central importance of *relationship* in counseling. Only in an atmosphere of safety will a person openly look at himself and consider changing beliefs which for years have determined his route to personal worth. The counseling office must be a safe place where the client knows he is accepted as a person regardless of his problems. Christians would do well to read Carl Rogers on the need for profoundly accepting the client as a worthwhile human being. In one place Rogers said: "I launch myself into the therapeutic relationship, having a hypothesis, or faith, that my liking, my confidence, my understanding of the other person's inner world will lead to a significant process of becoming . . . I enter the relationship as a person."[3]

In this kind of relationship, people are best able to face themselves and change.

Think for a moment. Where do you feel safe? With whom could you totally open up without fear of criticism or rejection, confident that you would be accepted and that the other person would make a genuine attempt to understand you? It is that kind of relationship which counseling should ideally provide in order to facilitate change in deeply and emotionally held wrong beliefs.

Basic Direction (Heart)

A third element in the human personality involves the basic direction a person chooses for himself. Scripture often speaks of the heart of man. The Greek word *kardia* is used in so many different ways that it is difficult to assign to it one central meaning. Literally, of course, it refers to the chief organ of physical life.

Scripture teaches that " . . . the life of the flesh is in the blood" (Lev. 17:11) and the heart fulfills the function of keeping the body supplied with a life-giving supply of blood. Vine states that, "By an easy transition the word came to stand for man's entire mental and moral activity, both the rational and emotional elements. In other words, the heart is used figuratively for the hidden springs of the *personal* (italics mine) life."[4]

Underlying wrong thinking in the unconscious mind is the fact that the human personality as a whole is headed in the wrong direction. Apart from God's sovereign work, people ultimately are out for themselves. All of their capacities (rationality, moral judgment, emotions, will) working together move toward the sinful goal of self-exaltation: "I want to serve me; I want what I want and when I want it; I want things the way I like." If the heart is a broad term including our entire personal nature and if it does refer to the " . . . hidden springs of our personal life," then perhaps the heart as used in Scripture is that essential part of the person which chooses his basic direction in life. Said in another way, I am suggesting the heart represents a person's fundamental intentions: for whom or what do I choose to live?

Someone has said that when the range of possible answers to a question has been carefully thought through, it becomes rather narrow. From a biblical perspective, there really are only two possible basic directions which one may choose: live for self or live for God. If with your heart you choose to live for self (which we all naturally do), then you will never have your personal needs fully met. By cutting God off (what a staggering concept of freedom — mere humans can cut God off from their lives), you cut off the only source of true significance and security. You then are left to yourself and so you do the best you can in meeting your personal needs. You may sift through the options available within the world, and, perhaps with the help of a therapist, reject some of the more obviously neurotic ones (for example, I will be secure only if everyone likes me all the time), but you will not find an option that will fully and completely satisfy your needs. Without bringing

God into the picture you are left with selecting from the various alternatives supplied by the devil through a false world system. The person who with his heart is serving self looks like this.

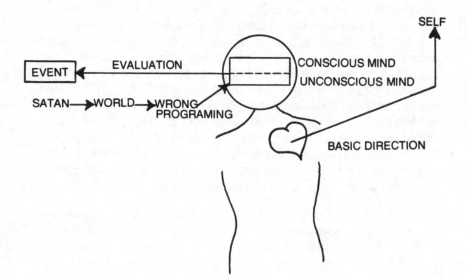

If, however, your basic intention is, by God's grace, to put Christ first and to serve Him, then you can *reject all of the world's ideas* on how to become worthwhile (and good riddance to them — none of them work) and you can start filling your conscious mind with the truths of Scripture. When I was teaching this concept to a group recently, without forethought I shouted that we must "Fill our *nous* with biblical truths." The Christian whose heart is truly committed to Christ would then look like this.

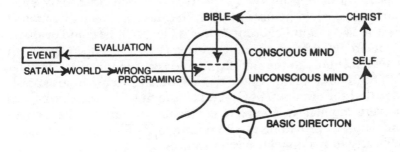

Rather than *eliminating* self, this person has understood that one is to *lose* self in Christ. "Not my will, but thine"; "I am crucified with Christ: nevertheless I live; yet not I, but Christ liveth in me"; "Whosoever will lose his life for my sake, the same shall save it"; "that in all things he might have the preeminence." Now there are two sources of input into the conscious mind: what Satan says through the world to our unconscious mind and what God says through the Bible to our conscious mind. If the individual's propositional response to events still draws from his unconsciously held wrong assumptions, he will function no more effectively than the unbeliever. But, if he renews his mind by evaluating events from a biblical perspective, he will become a transformed person. When the event of disapproval presents itself, he will *make himself say* on the authority of Scripture, "My security and significance as a person depend only upon my relationship to Christ. Although I don't enjoy this rejection at all, still my worth as a person is untouched. Therefore this event is painful but not devastating. I know God can work for good through this

99

difficult event so I can keep going, trust Him, respond biblically, and not crumble."

Paul looked at events in his life from God's perspective. When confined unfairly to jail, he was able to evaluate that event as perhaps regrettable and certainly uncomfortable but as one in which God could work (Phil. 1:12-18). His significance did not depend on having his own way. It rather depended only upon knowing he could be used of God. Because the basic direction of his heart was right ("For me to live is Christ"), he could evaluate events from God's perspective and experience the deep joy which is available only to the significant and secure individual. He was significant as a servant of the living God and secure in his knowledge that the omnipotent God was his loving Shepherd, who was at every moment in complete control of all that was happening and who was providing all the resources Paul needed to respond biblically to his difficult circumstances.

Will

In addition to the conscious mind, the unconscious mind, and the heart, people have a capacity for choosing how they behave. Any concept of personal functioning which left out the *will* would be incomplete. The New Testament has at least two root words (*boule* and *thelema*) which convey the notion of choice. People generally *choose* to do what makes sense to them. In other words, perceptions or evaluations about life (what one tells himself in his conscious mind) determine the range of behavior within which people choose to perform. A person's freedom of choice is restricted by the limits of his rational understanding. The thorny issue of free will must be discussed with an awareness of the fact that people choose to do only what they understand to be sensible. For example, the problem with an unsaved person is not his inability to choose God. His will is perfectly capable of choosing to trust Christ, but his darkened understanding will not allow his

100

will to make that choice. He does not need a strengthened will; he needs an enlightened mind, and that is the work of the Holy Spirit.

Preachers and counselors can spend their energy exhorting people to change their behavior. But the human will is not a free entity. It is bound to a person's understanding. People will do what they believe. Rather than making a concerted effort to influence choices, preachers first need to be influencing minds. When a person *understands* who Christ is, on what basis he is worthwhile, and what life is all about, he has the formulation necessary for any sustained change in life style. Christians who try to "live right" without correcting a wrong understanding about how to meet personal needs will always labor and struggle with Christianity, grinding out their responsible duty in a joyless, strained fashion. Christ taught that when we *know the truth*, we can be set free. We now are *free* to choose the life of obedience because we understand that in Christ we now are worthwhile persons. We are *free* to express our gratitude in the worship and service of the One who has met our needs.

It must be stressed that obedience does not *automatically* follow from correct understanding. Remember, I said that our perceptions determine the *range* of options we can choose. The will is a real part of the human personality with the function of *responsibly choosing* to behave consistently with how the Bible teaches us to evaluate our world. And such choices are not always easy. It often involves teeth-gritting effort to choose to behave as we should. It is important to choose to do what is right moment by moment. Apart from the clear exercise of the will, there will be no consistent obedience. As the Christian continues to choose the path of righteousness, his capacity for right choices in the face of adversity and temptation enlarges. He becomes a stronger Christian, one whom God can trust with greater responsibilities.

Our sketch of psycho-anatomy must include this important element.

101

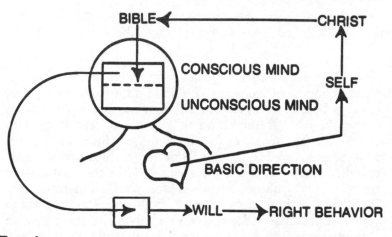

Emotions

One more part of the human personality will make our drawing complete, and that is our capacity for feeling, our emotions. By discussing the emotions last I do not mean to imply that how a person feels is unimportant. My strong emphasis on thinking may create the wrong impression that as long as a person thinks right, a counselor should be satisfied. I do believe that right thinking is a necessary foundation for right feeling. As I expressed in my first book, counseling can be thought of as an effort to learn "right thinking," to choose "right behaviors," and then to experience "right feelings."

The Scriptures say much about feelings. We read that the Lord often was moved to compassion as He encountered human need. He felt deep caring emotions. The Greek word translated compassion in the Gospels (*splagchnon*) is rendered "bowels" or affections in the Epistles. John speaks of shutting up the bowels of compassion when you do not respond helpfully to a brother or sister in need. Such a person might be called a "constipated Christian."

Christians often are confused about this whole subject of feelings. Some give the impression that if you walk with the Lord, confessing all known sin, then you will always feel good. Others

102

teach that it is possible for a Christian to have negative emotions, but they must be kept under lock and key and never expressed. To these people, unhappy emotions are a shameful blight on Christian testimony and therefore must never be seen. Such teaching produces spiritual phonies. We all feel bad sometimes. And all "bad" feelings are not morally bad. Some negative feelings, even though excruciating, are perfectly acceptable and normal experiences in the Christian walk and can coexist with a deep sense of peace and joy. Other negative emotions result from sinful thinking and living. But even these should not be hushed up and buried, but should rather be dealt with by examining their causes and doing something constructive to remedy the problem.

If some negative feelings are acceptable and some stem from sin, how do we tell which are which? I want to propose that the criterion for distinguishing between non-sin-related negative emotions and sin-related ones is this: *any feeling which is mutually exclusive with compassion involves sin.* The major feeling in a spiritual, Christ-centered life is the deep, gut-level feeling of compassion for others. Paul reminded the Galatians that after they met the Lord they cared so much about Paul that they gladly would have given him their own eyes. Apparently Paul suffered from an eye disease which prompted the Galatians to sacrificial compassion. They really cared about the problems of their brother. What a rebuke to me. I might have been willing to foot the bill for a trip to the eye doctor, but donate my eyes? That's asking a little much. And yet that level of concern characterized those early Christians who were filled with the love of Christ. Now the point is this: any emotion that blocks the development or thwarts the expression of this kind of compassion involves sin. Negative emotions which in no way interfere with feelings of compassion are acceptable. Incidentally, a good barometer of your fellowship with the Lord is your level of compassion for a lost world and a suffering church.

Christianity was never intended to be one laugh after another. The abundant life which Christians walk down countless aisles to find is not the comfortable, problem-free existence most are hoping to receive. It is a life of warfare, a struggle for God

103

against Satan, a life full of disappointments, heartaches, and suffering. So what is abundant about it? Simply this: the knowledge that we belong to the God of reality, that we are living a meaningful life under the guidance and control of a caring Savior who one day will bring us into eternal rest. Christians who fail to understand this sometimes feel guilty and question their Christian profession if they aren't consciously happy all the time. I have come to dislike the light, frivolous songs which promise "happiness all the time" and prefer the solid hymns which bring out the attributes of God, His eternal plans, and His loving provisions for His children. Paul certainly wasn't bubbly all the time. Christ Himself knew what it was to feel anger and loneliness and anguish. If our Lord experienced painful emotions, and if a spiritual giant like Paul felt them as well, then we should not be surprised if we go through exceedingly painful times.

Perhaps a few examples will be helpful. In Column A I have listed a few negative emotions which block compassion and therefore involve sin. The non-sinful counterpart to each appears in Column B with a Scripture reference in which that particular emotion is illustrated.

Column A	Column B
1. *Depression:* self-preoccupation, self-pity, giving up. No concern for others; therefore no action on behalf of others.	1. *Anguish:* deep hurt over difficult circumstances, emotional pain over loss, soul-searching agony as problems mount. Luke 22:44
2. *Crippling Guilt:* feelings of worthlessness and self-punishment which do not lead to positive steps to correct the problem. Such feelings often serve as an excuse from working responsibly on problem areas.	2. *Constructive Sorrow:* In their excellent book *Guilt and Freedom*, Bruce Narramore and Bill Counts describe an attitude of contrition and sorrow over misdeeds which leads to changed behavior. 2 Corinthians 7:8-10.
3. *Resentment:* holding a	3. *Anger:* reaction to moral

104

grudge, letting many suns go down upon your wrath, behavior motivated by vengeance.

wrong which asserts holiness of God and rebukes sin with eye toward vindicating God's holiness and restoring the offender to right behavior. Matthew 21:12,13. *Jesus in temple*

4. *Frustration:* a "throwing up of the hands" attitude, what's the use of trying, frantic effort to change, smoldering anger at unchanging problems.

4. *Motivated Discontent:* concern with difficult circumstances which leads to either a plan to change them or, if that proves impossible, an attitude of accepting something unpleasant knowing God can work in every situation. Philippians 1:12. *Paul*

✝5. *Anxiety:* apprehension about anticipated unpleasant event either specific or vague which is so strong that it controls behavior; e.g., preoccupying worry over how someone will respond to me.

5. *Concern:* anticipation of possible future event which does not cause disobedience to God, but rather provokes intelligent forethought. Proverbs 6:6-11.

In every instance, the wrong negative emotion can be traced to a wrong assumption about how personal needs can be met. That point will become clearer in chapter 6. Let me say here that if I rightly understand the basis for regarding myself as worthwhile, I will evaluate whatever happens to me in such a way that I will not feel depression, crippling guilt, resentment, frustration, or anxiety. Each of these emotions springs from deficit motivation which in turn is caused by wrong thinking. Anxiety, resentment, and guilt are the basic problem conditions behind all other personal difficulties. If I believe that all I need is God and what He chooses to provide, I will not experience any of these three emotions. *Guilt* comes from believing that what God provides is not enough and then going outside of God's will to secure what He has not provided. *Resentment* comes from believing that my needs are threatened by something which He has allowed to happen to me. *Anxiety* is the fear that something I need will not be provided.

How we think not only determines the range of behavior from which we may choose, it also greatly influences how we feel. If our thinking is based on the world's wrong value system, we will experience negative emotions which will block compassion. If, however, our thinking is based on Scripture, we will evaluate events in such a way that, although we may feel painful emotions, a deep, real care and compassion will continue to be expressed. Only a Christian whose needs are met in Christ is capable of sustained compassion, no matter what the circumstances. Our Lord therefore taught that the distinguishing mark of the Christian should be love, expressed by a community of believers getting along on the basis of genuine concern for each other.

Our sketch of psycho-anatomy can now be completed. First, let's look at the personal insides of the unbeliever.

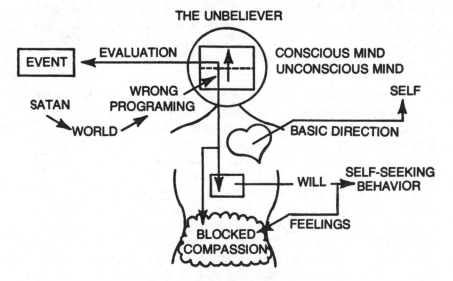

THE UNBELIEVER

Chart 8 in Appendix

Unbeliever

He is out for himself; he evaluates his life in terms of the world's value system; he behaves in a manner designed to meet his own needs; he does not genuinely care for others — all because he has believed the devil's lie about how to be a person. He is truly a son of Satan. But look at the committed believer.

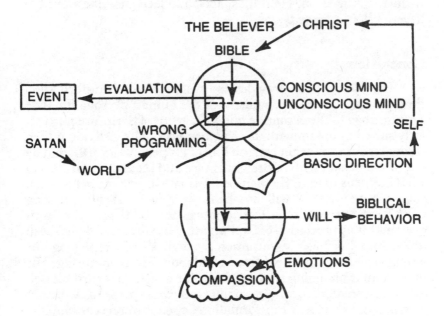

Chart 9 in Appendix

Notice that the wrong beliefs he has learned still enter his conscious mind but he deliberately evaluates his world from a biblical framework. Notice too that the arrow between Behavior and Compassion points both ways: the more compassion I feel, the more compassionately I'll behave and the more I choose to behave compassionately, the more compassion I'll feel. The Christian's purpose is to live for Christ. He evaluates his life from God's perspective; he chooses to behave as God tells him to; he feels compassion for others and behaves accordingly. This man experiences a deep sense of his own personal worth and knows experientially the fruit of the Spirit. A Christian living as a carnal man is still living for himself, still evaluating his world from a false perspective, and he therefore behaves selfishly, disobediently, and without compassion. He thinks, acts, and feels just like an unbeliever. What a tragedy.

Conclusion

The Holy Spirit provides the resources for transformation through the normal mechanisms of the human personality. The Spirit brings to the receptive mind the truth of Scripture particularly suited to the immediate circumstances. The individual then recognizes that no event can rob him of his personal worth, that he is a whole person with both significance and security regardless of what happens to him. He then can evaluate the events in his life in such a way that he will not behave or feel selfishly (moving OVER). As he continues to evaluate events biblically, the Spirit deepens his appreciation of God's truth. His Christian beliefs seep down into his basic assumption system, slowly replacing the wrong beliefs he has held from childhood. He is maturing. His inner man is changing (moving UP). He comes to regard himself as a non-threatened, whole person who can express his worth in worship and service. Transformation depends upon renewing the mind.

Notes

[1]Phenomenology: to understand a person you must know how the world appears to him. Objectivism: to understand a person you must know what his world is.
[2]W. E. Vine, *An Expository Dictionary of New Testament Words* (Old Tappan, New Jersey: Revell, 1966).
[3]Carl R. Rogers, "Learning to be Free," an unpublished paper cited in Dugald

Personality Structure

S. Arbuckle, *Counseling: Philosophy, Theory, and Practice,* second edition (Boston: Allyn and Bacon, Inc., 1970).
    [4]*Expository Dictionary.*

**PART III: BASIC STRATEGY: HOW TO UNDERSTAND
AND DEAL WITH PERSONAL PROBLEMS**

CHAPTER 6

How Problems Develop I

Without a clear understanding of how problems develop, counseling can become nothing more than a warm, friendly conversation full of good intentions. In the back of many counselors' minds, hidden behind a hopefully confident, relaxed appearance, the question rumbles, "What on earth can I say that might be helpful?" If the counselor has just read a book on Rogerian counseling, he is likely to warmly grunt, "I understand," hoping that his client will believe him. If his most recent reading was *Competent to Counsel* by Jay Adams,[1] he perhaps would look for an opportunity to forcefully assert that "It is sinful to do that. You must repent and change. Here are the Scriptures to read which will help you." Professional and pastoral counselors alike tend to rely on a few techniques and two or three basic principles, perhaps without ever clearly thinking through exactly why their counseling efforts should work.

In this chapter I want to draw together many of the thoughts presented so far into a model of human behavior. If a counselor has a widely applicable conception of how people develop problems, he will have a better chance of understanding his client and will try rationally to solve the problems according to a systematic and intelligent strategy. To some degree man will forever remain a mystery. Who can exhaustively understand the product of an infinite God? However, a good, clear model explaining the basics of human functioning can deliver us from a "hit or miss, let's hope this helps" approach and lend at least a measure of precision to our counseling efforts. The model I have in mind is sketched easily. I find it useful to keep the sketch in my mind as I counsel, attempting to fit the problem I am dealing with into the model, to thus better understand what to do with it. Let me develop the sketch by introducing each element singly.

The first concept in the model is *need*. Because people are both physical beings and personal beings, they have both physical needs and personal needs. Physical needs consist of whatever is needed to physically survive, to keep the body alive — food, clothing, shelter, etc. Personal needs consist of whatever is required to personally survive, to keep the person alive — significance and security as a basis for self-worth. We must have purpose and love if we are to remain alive as persons. Many people are in the process of dying and do not realize their plight. As long as they entertain the hope that more money, fame, prestige, sex, travel, whatever will provide them with significance and security, they keep going. As soon as they face the horrid blackness of no worth and no hope of attaining it, a deep, overwhelming despair sets in. At that point they either suicide, have a nervous breakdown, become psychotically withdrawn or bizarre, or plunge into irrational efforts to dull the pain (alcohol, drugs, running away, pornography, etc.). When a person grasps the truth that he is significant and secure in Christ and begins to practice that truth by rational, responsible, obedient, and committed living, he becomes whole, alive, vibrant, full. Life, no matter how difficult the circumstances, is worth the living. It makes sense. There is reason to go on. All the characteristics of a self-actualizing, mature personality begin to emerge.

Psychologists make an important distinction between pri-

mary needs and secondary needs. The primary personal needs are
significance and security. Secondary needs (sometimes called
acquired needs) are simply those things in our life which have
been the means of meeting our primary needs. Psychologist B. F.
Skinner has technically defined a secondary reinforcer (or need)
as a stimulus event which has acquired its reinforcing property
through prior service as a discriminative stimulus.

Let me say that again a little more simply. A green light tells
me that now is the time I should cross the street with a good
chance of getting across safely. The green light then is a discriminative stimulus, something which discriminates or marks
the time when I can meet my primary need (in this case physical
safety as I cross the street). As I wait at the corner I notice a
button which when pressed makes the light turn green. I find
myself motivated to press the button because I want to produce
the event of a green light. But why do I value a green light, apart
from possible aesthetic preference? It has no independent or
primary value at all. A green light meets no need within me. But it
does allow me the *opportunity* to meet the primary need of physical
survival as I cross the street. The green light then has a secondary
or acquired value. I need the green light not because it directly
meets my needs but because it allows me to meet my needs.
Money is another obvious example of a discriminative stimulus
which has become an acquired need. A piece of green paper is
not edible. It cannot meet my hunger need. But with it I can buy
food which will satisfy my hunger. Therefore I *learn* to "need"
money.

I have labored the point because counselors must clearly
understand the difference between primary personal needs and
acquired (culturally taught) personal needs. Clients often will
claim to *need* approval from others. But they don't. What they do
in fact *need* is security. It may be that all their lives a feeling of
security has depended upon the approval of other people. A
strong parent can so overwhelm a child that he spends his entire
life trying to please people in order to enjoy the good fellowship
associated with mother's approval. But if this person could see

that what he really needs is not approval but security, he might then consider other possible ways to meet that need. The key is the recognition that he does not need approval; he needs security. Approval is an acquired need, security is primary. People can never stop needing significance and security. *But we can stop needing certain acquired routes to satisfying our primary needs of significance and security (1) if these routes create problems and (2) if there is a problem-free route to meeting those same primary needs.*

Counselors must differentiate between *needs* and *wants*. We *need* significance and security in order to persevere in faithful living. We may *want* approval, money, fame, recognition, promotion, new home, a good marriage, improved looks, smaller nose, better personality, slimmer figure, business success, big car, kids that turn out well, friends, an effective ministry, etc., etc. And I may passionately want them to the point where their absence provokes a nonsinful legitimate pain of excruciating proportions. But I do not *need* any of them in order to be a whole person who can live biblically. I can live a deeply meaningful and personally whole life without satisfying my wants, although that life may be riddled with anguish. Paul is a prime example. But neither Paul nor I can continue to function effectively for Christ without satisfying our *needs*. I refer the reader to my first book for a discussion of what really meets my needs.

The first concept then is *needs*, not wants, not acquired needs, not secondary reinforcers, but *needs*. In a model of how a person functions, we begin with the personal needs of significance and security.

The second concept in the model is *motivation*. Simply stated, motivation is the drive or urge to meet my needs. It is that sense of momentum which impels me to do something to become significant and secure. As a fallen people we experience an acute, keen desire to be significant and secure. We are willing to expend tremendous personal energy in an effort to satisfy these needs. We call this profound, compulsive willingness to meet needs motivation. So far the model looks like this.

Motivation considered by itself is little more than random,

START HERE:

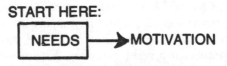

Refer to Chart 10 in Appendix

undifferentiated energy. I am willing to do something, to move, to work hard at becoming a worthwhile person. But what do I do? In what direction do I choose to move? What am I motivated to do? What becomes important to me? In what pursuits do I expend my motivational energy? The answer to these questions is as important as it is simple: *the direction which I am motivated to follow in an effort to meet my needs depends neither on the needs nor on the motivational energy but rather on what I think will meet those needs*. The needs are there and I am anxious to meet them, so I am motivated to do whatever I *believe* will give me significance and security.

Children pass through a variety of developmental stages. Millard Sall, in his book *Faith, Psychology and Christian Maturity*, gives an excellent, readable summary of the psychoanalytic view of the stages in personal growth. In each of these stages a child is motivated to find some way to meet his personal needs. At some point he hits upon a strategy which seems to work. Perhaps he notices what other people regard as important. If dad continually talks about his athletic accomplishments, junior might decide that excellence in a specific area is the route to significance. If mother grumbles about father but continues working like a slave preparing his meals, cleaning his house, and washing his clothes, then daughter may learn that security is supposed to come from marriage but rarely does. As an adult she may decide to avoid the inevitable disappointment by staying single. Or if she does marry, she may quickly take an offensive position to protect herself from the hurt she anticipates. As soon as she sees something negative in her husband (a frown, coming home late, a comment about the untidy house), she automatically and unconsciously will interpret it as the expected rejection and respond with attack: "What do you mean the house is a mess? If you would pick up one finger to help me, maybe I could keep it straight. I have kids to look after, meals to cook, rugs to vacuum, and I'm trying as hard as I can and all you can do is blow up." At that point she might either burst into tears or maintain a rigid coolness. Either way she is trying desperately to avoid the hurt of insecurity. The root problem is a set of wrong assumptions about security which she learned as a child. Although the woman is responsible and accountable for her sinful attitudes and behavior, changing into a confident, secure Christian woman will depend on learning a new set of assumptions.

Although I am unclear as to precisely how a child selects his strategies for finding personal worth, it seems reasonable to suggest that he is influenced primarily by whatever consistent pattern of living his parents display. Proverbs 22:6 tells us to train up our children in the way they should go. The Hebrew word for "train up" first was used (according to Howard Hendricks in his superb material on child training) to refer to a Hebrew midwife placing her finger in the mouth of the newborn infant in order to stimulate the sucking reflex. The general thought contained in the word is to do something which triggers basic reflexes, to prompt a natural activity, or even more broadly, to create a desire. Children are naturally motivated to meet their personal needs. The job of parents is to prompt that basic reflex by the way we live. We are to create a desire in our children to look to the Lord for the satisfaction of their personal (as well as physical) needs. Make no mistake. Children will in some form reproduce our efforts to find significance and security. If we really believe that money or achievement brings significance or that compliments and attractive clothing bring security, we can prate all we want about the joys of knowing Jesus. Our kids will learn to depend on what we really are depending on for our satisfaction in life. No amount of teaching, family devotions, or trips to church will effectively counter the message we convey by our lives. Children will learn that their needs can be met if they reach the same goal for which their parents strive.

In our day youngsters are more and more recognizing that

118

the goals to which their parents have dedicated their lives (money, prestige, good jobs, etc.) do not satisfy. Hard work for the sake of hard work as a value in itself is seen to be empty. And it is. The goals which typically beckon us are in reality artificial and unsatisfying. They do not provide what people desperately need, real significance (a purpose for living) or real security (a valid sense of being loved). Children up to a certain age implicitly accept their parents' ideologies. But our generation has encouraged young people to begin questioning. And that is good. When they become teens, many turn away from the ambitions of their parents, correctly seeing only futility in their pursuit.

The tragedy is that they often exchange one error for another as they steadily gravitate toward mystical, irrational, experiential strategies for finding some satisfaction — drugs, free sex, occultism, adventure, anything. The premium today is on finding something that feels good. Admonishing these kids to straighten up and get a responsible job is worse than useless. It is insensitive to the problem. The church of Jesus Christ needs to hold out the reality of true significance and security by our unswerving and uncompromising commitment to the absolutes of Scripture and by our *practice* (not merely our expression) of unconditional love. Unless these people find the rational, legitimate answer to their deepest needs which only Christianity affords, they will become either machine-like puppets, mechanically conforming to society's expectations (Is that what we really want, down deep? It may be.) or they will plunge into the horrible blackness of utter despair — no meaning, no love, no nothing; moving on as zombies going nowhere or, if they have the courage, committing suicide.

I wonder if the sins of the parents are passed on to children (Exod. 34:7) when the children learn from their parents' example false notions about where to find significance and security. I thank God for parents who taught my brother and me by their lives as well as by their words that trusting in the Lord and living for Him was the foundation for all effective living. The clear challenge for parents is to live in such a way that we truly do depend on the

119

Lord for our significance and security.

Children will develop a strategy for meeting their needs. The world (primarily their parents), the flesh (their own innate resistance to seeking after God, Rom. 3:10-13), and the devil (who delights to offer any god which does not include submission to Christ) combine to teach the child a false basic assumption about how personal needs can be met. Usually people develop one broad, guiding idea. Examples that I commonly see in my practice are: "I will be significant if

— I have money
— I excel
— I never make a mistake
— I am a steady worker
— my kids turn out well
— I am granted recognition by my peer group
— I am included in important circles."

"I will be secure if

— I have a loving husband
— I am never criticized (an assumption which underlies perfectionism: "If I'm perfect, I can't be criticized").
— everyone accepts me
— no one frowns or hollers or in some way rejects me."

When children latch onto a basic assumption, their motivation acquires direction. A goal is set. They now will engage in behavior designed to meet the goal which their basic assumption has determined. Our sketch can now be expanded.

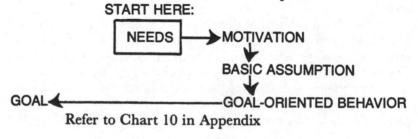

START HERE:

NEEDS ——→ MOTIVATION

BASIC ASSUMPTION

GOAL ◄———————————— GOAL-ORIENTED BEHAVIOR

Refer to Chart 10 in Appendix

The diagram as it now looks suggests one way in which problems develop. Goal-oriented behavior can be intelligent, realistic, and sensible or it can be ignorant, unrealistic, and utterly ineffective. The goal therefore may not be reached, the person will feel threatened as his needs remain unmet, and he will become anxious or resentful. For example, if a wife believes that her fundamental security depends upon her husband's loving her, she likely will try to reach the goal of winning her husband's love. But perhaps she does not understand what turns a man on. She may help him with his business or she may take over family budgeting and do it efficiently, but neglect keeping herself trim or warmly greeting him when he comes home. Problems develop in this marriage. Her husband is cool to her. The goal is not reached. When she consults the counselor, hurt and bitter, complaining about her unaffectionate, distant husband, she may come to understand what she is doing wrong. Her goal-oriented behavior is ignorant and ineffective. So she runs to the local bookstore and picks up a few books on becoming a complete woman, a sizzling sex partner, a feminine delight. In an attempt to win his love she learns to cook special meals, she admires his body, wears sexy lingerie and cute, frilly dresses, and on and on and on.

Now let me quickly insist that I haven't a single objection when my wife does all the above. I like it. More women should give it a try. But there are two real problems with a counseling approach which seeks only to change irrational goal-oriented behavior into more intelligent and effective efforts to achieve the same goal.

(1) The goal of winning her husband's love may be absolutely unreachable no matter what the desperate wife tries to do. If so, then what? Is she doomed to insecurity until her husband changes or until she can find another man to love her?

(2) The wife's basic motivation is self-centered. All the advice on how to be an effective woman has simply taught this

121

woman how to more effectively manipulate her husband to meet her needs.

A wife with an unfulfilled need operates from deficit motivation. She is at the center of her world trying to fill her emptiness.

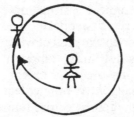

In the above diagram the arrow pointing to the husband represents the wife's behavior toward him. The arrow from her husband back to her indicates the desired outcome of her efforts, namely his loving her. She is giving to get. In reality, she is doing nothing more than *using* her husband to meet her needs.

Christian marriage is different. Perhaps it could be sketched like this.

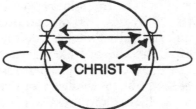

In this diagram of an ideal marriage, the Lord is meeting the basic needs in each spouse. Both now are full and operating therefore from Expression Motivation. Their behavior toward each other is giving for the purpose of helping the other become closer to Christ. The wife may be doing most of the things the books told her to do, but now her motivation is different. She longs to see him come closer to Christ. If he loves her in return, that's icing on the cake. Although icing is sweet and makes the cake much more appealing, it's not the central, most substantial element. If he does not love her, she remains secure and desires to minister to him as God directs and so she continues to willingly submit, praying that God will use her behavior to bring him closer to the Lord.

Problems then can develop at the point of goal-oriented behavior. People can move effectively or ineffectively toward their goal. Counseling which helps a person reach a goal determined by a wrong assumption actually amounts to teaching a tick how to more productively drain a dog. If a client can be helped to reach a goal through more effective strategies, he will achieve a measure of satisfaction. But if it is true that only Christ can truly satisfy our needs and if the client's goal was determined by a wrong assumption about what brings significance and security, the client who reaches his goal will not be thoroughly satisfied, his needs still will be unmet, and he will be motivated to go through the cycle again and reach new goals. All his life he will chase after things which never satisfy. God told Jeremiah that His people " . . . have forsaken me the fountain of living waters, and hewed them out cisterns, broken cisterns, that can hold no water" (Jer. 2:13).

Our Lord told the Samaritan woman that people who rely on any source of nourishment other than Christ Himself will never be content. The cycle of drawing water from the well becomes perpetual, wearisome labor, continually toiling for that which never satisfies. What a tragedy to see men locked into a corporate structure, sacrificing their families to "make it" in business. An expensive home with a Rolls Royce in the garage and a bank account that is bulging amount to nothing more than a broken cistern. Paul knew how to abound and how to be abased. He could enjoy luxuries if they came his way but he also could do without them. He realized that depending on material possessions for happiness was like lowering a bucket into an empty well in order to satisfy thirst. Material possessions hold no water which can nourish the soul with true significance and security, but so often people get a longer rope to drop the bucket deeper into the bottomless, waterless well, hoping that eventually they will find what they seek. Others give up on the life of affluence, sell everything, and move to a fishing village or a farm in the country, all in an effort to quiet that uneasy sense of dull, aching emptiness. Many people cannot afford either to buy more things or move to the country, but longingly imagine that if they could, their needs would be met. However nothing apart from relationship with Christ will ever satisfy.

Let me now add to the diagram.

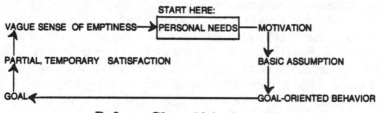

Refer to Chart 10 in Appendix

The diagram now reflects how most "well-adjusted" people live. They have set goals for themselves according to unbiblical assumptions about how needs can be met. Through hard work, careful planning, or "dumb luck" (many would call it that), they have reached their goals. They have money, nice kids, good health, business prestige, whatever they value, and they enjoy a real measure of personal prosperity and happiness. These folks don't consult psychologists. Some feel no need for God in their lives. They're doing fine without Him. An insistence that their deepest needs remain unmet and are aching for satisfaction often falls on deaf ears. The problem is that when everything goes according to plan people really do feel good. The way that seems right has been achieved and is bringing temporary satisfaction. It is hard to convince these folks that the end of their way is personal death — eternity with neither meaning nor love.

There are some people who, when they reach all their goals, are brought face to face with the horrible fact that "dreams come true" have not really satisfied. Marilyn Monroe had everything most girls yearn for: good looks, well-proportioned figure, men galore, fame, money, glamour. Yet she killed herself. Why? She apparently reached the pitiable but honest stage of utter despair: "I've reached all my goals but they don't satisfy. I'm empty. Life is not worth the living. There's nothing else to try. I've tried everything. Nothing relieves that deep pain inside me. Death is now the only possible relief." Adding this kind of experience to our diagram, it now looks like this.

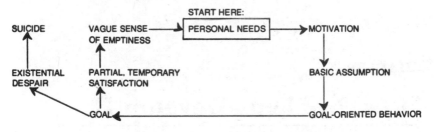

Refer to Chart 10 in Appendix

So far I have sketched a simple model of human behavior and suggested a few ways in which problems develop. In the next chapter I will add one more key element to the model, the element which is directly responsible for most of the problems which appear in a counselor's office.

Notes

[1]Jay Adams, *Competent to Counsel* (Grand Rapids: Baker, 1970).

CHAPTER 7

How Problems Develop II

A person comes to see you. "I get such headaches. The doctor says nothing is wrong with me physically but my head sure hurts. I know I'm tense. But if these are really tension headaches, I don't know what to do. Can you help?"

What would you say to your client? Perhaps you're a pastor or an elder or perhaps a Christian in the body whom this individual trusts. Many would be tempted to say, "Look, this sounds like a psychosomatic problem which frankly is beyond my abilities to handle. Have you considered seeing a psychologist?" Others might encourage behaviors designed to aid relaxation ("Do you have a hobby?" "How about propping up your feet and tuning out the world?") Some might unwisely recommend transcendental meditation, unaware of its insidious pull toward a godless view of life. Perhaps the counselor would try to identify the source of tension and help the person deal with it biblically.

As I indicated at the beginning of chapter 6, intelligent counseling requires a good conceptual understanding of how the problem developed. Physicians are taught the maxim: diagnosis first, then treatment. How do you diagnose this problem? Diagnosis to me simply means understanding what caused the problem and what is maintaining it.

In the last chapter I put into diagram form the idea that people are motivated to reach whatever goal they assume will meet their deepest personal needs. I now want to expand the model to explain how many psychological problems develop. *The key element behind most symptoms is an obstacle which interferes with reaching the individual's chosen goal.* If the obstacle can be overcome by making changes in goal-oriented behavior, the threat of neurosis is averted. But, as was pointed out in the last chapter, if the goal is based on unbiblical assumptions, the result is either partial satisfaction — and more treadmill-style chasing after fulfillment — or despair. Sometimes the obstacle cannot be overcome ("I can't get my husband to love me." "No matter how hard I try, I keep making mistakes.") Most often these stubborn obstacles which remain standing despite the best efforts of frustrated people fall into one of three categories:

Category #1: Unreachable Goals
Category #2: External Circumstances
Category #3: Fear of Failure

Whenever someone encounters an obstacle on the road to a desperately desired goal, they experience frustration. The emotional form which the frustration assumes depends on the nature of the obstacle encountered. If the goal set by the individual is unreachable (Category #1), the most usual primary emotional response is *guilt* or feelings of self-derogation. If the person believes that his goal is reachable (whether it is or not) but that some external circumstance has blocked the path to the goal (Category #2), the result is typically *resentment*. If the block is neither an unreachable goal nor a thwarting circumstance but a disabling fear of failure (Category #3), the person usually experiences *anxiety*.

The three problem emotions behind most of our personal

difficulties are guilt, anxiety, and resentment. In order to better understand how each of these develops from a specific kind of frustrating experience, let me briefly discuss the three kinds of obstacles leading to these three separate emotions.

Category #1: Unreachable Goals

Certain goals which people set for themselves simply cannot be reached no matter how hard they try. Some people think (Basic Assumption) that the only way to feel good about themselves is to avoid all criticism. One middle-aged woman I worked with had been put down consistently by her mother, unfavorably compared to her sister by both parents, and generally harangued by everyone. A diet of constant criticism produces a bad case of emotional indigestion in a child. This woman came to believe that good feelings about herself (security) depended on never being criticized. In order to avoid all criticism, she had to live perfectly. Her objective became the *unreachable goal* of perfection. She married a fine man who truly loved and accepted her. But she made mistakes. She overcooked the soft-boiled eggs, forgot to do the laundry which left her husband without clean underwear, overspent her food budget, etc. On occasion her husband would criticize, usually patiently, gently, and constructively. She was shattered. She couldn't blame her husband because he was so obviously supportive and kind. The fault was entirely hers. As a consequence she hated herself and mercilessly attacked herself with biting invectives and despairing remorse. No amount of support or encouragement would help. In fact, loving concern seemed to make matters worse: the kinder her world was, the more she realized that the fault was hers, that she was imperfect.

Psychologists reading this will suspect that in addition to her guilt (which in this case amounted to a realized fear of rejection), there probably was a substantial measure of anger against her world (primarily her husband) for requiring perfection. Although the resentment may be primary, I am inclined to think that guilt is the larger problem whenever there is a self-imposed unattainable

128

standard against which a person measures himself. If the client accepts responsibility for not reaching his unreachable goal, he feels unworthy. Often these feelings are expressed in statements of self-hatred, attitudes of despairing disgust with oneself, and a loss of motivation to try.

Category #2: External Circumstances

A different situation exists when the client perceives that the goal would be reachable if it were not for blocks outside of himself. In that event the primary problem emotion is resentment. In my judgment, the most common problem behind the variety of concerns I deal with in my office is resentment.

The children of Israel offer instructive examples of this emotional problem. Whenever difficult circumstances arose, they repeatedly murmured against Moses, complaining about how badly things were going for them. Their resentment against unpleasant events in their lives boiled to the point that they were ready to stone Moses, the man they blamed for all their problems. Psychologists have long debated the "frustration-aggression hypothesis." According to the theory, aggression is the inevitable response to a frustrating agent. If I am trying to reach a goal but you frustrate my efforts by getting in the way, I will feel angry toward you. The Israelites' behavior appears to illustrate this idea. It seems to me, however, that the theory can be more precisely understood as follows: when someone perceives that his goal could have been reached if it were not for an interfering block of some sort (for which he does not feel responsible), he will feel aggressive resentment toward that block. If, however, the frustrating obstacle is not an external circumstance, but either an unreachable goal or fear of failure, the frustration will not yield angry aggression but rather will become either guilt or anxiety.

A middle-aged woman consulted me concerning severe headaches which had required intermittent hospitalization over a three-year period. Her psychiatrist had indicated possible organic brain problems and was treating her with enough medication to

129

justify a hotline to her druggist. In our first two or three interviews it became apparent that she was filled with anger against her mother for interfering in her life and against her husband for failing her emotionally for years. Her basic assumption was that in order to be secure she needed her family to accept her and strongly support her in all she did. When they became a block to her goal of strong support, she developed an intense bitterness toward them but was unable to express it for fear of further rejection. She continually tried to change both her mother and her husband to better fit her needs and, as usually happens when one person tries to change another, she failed completely. Her goal-oriented behavior was totally ineffective. The basis of her psychosomatic ailment was unexpressed resentment. She had violated the biblical principle to "let not the sun go down upon your wrath" (Eph. 4:26). The treatment, however, was not primarily a series of exhortations to behave biblically, but rather involved an exploration and radical alteration of her basic assumptions. As she learned that God's love was sufficient to meet her needs and then put that "unfelt belief" into practice by sharing her feelings with her husband and by giving up her need to change him, her headaches substantially disappeared.

Category #3: Fear of Failure

A third kind of block involves a fear of failure. American men often are gripped by this problem in their role as husband and father and, as a result, renege on their responsibilities. The goal may be reasonable and attainable. The path to the goal may be free from interference. But if someone is afraid he might not reach the goal, he often will waiver in anxious indecision. A husband desires a good marital relationship. He believes it is possible. His wife is willing and cooperative. But still he hesitates, suspended in a state of motionless indecision. Why? He is afraid he might make a mess of things, that his best efforts still would be substandard, so he does nothing. The premise on which he is operating is simple: if I try and fail, I will have to admit I'm a failure, and my self-concept couldn't stand that. If I never try, I can avoid failure. The truth is, of course, that never trying guarantees failure and is thus the worst option in the long run. Still he chooses that course because in the short run, he will not have to come face to face with his failure.

Miller and Dollard, two psychologists who have studied conflict, have developed a now classical diagram representing anxious indecision.

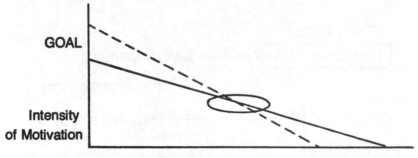

The vertical line represents the goal (getting a date, going for a job interview, accepting the responsibility to teach Sunday school, initiating a conversation with your spouse). At the starting point, the individual believes the goal is desirable and sets out to reach it. The solid gradually rising line is called the approach gradient. As he travels up the line toward the goal (walking to the phone to call the girl for a date), he finds himself wanting it more and more. His approach motivation becomes more intense. But as he continues to move toward the goal, he begins to feel a little uneasy (as he reaches for the phone, his stomach flutters a little, but still he picks it up). The broken line represents the avoidance gradient, the fear that he will not reach the goal (the girl might say no). He will continue to move toward the goal until he reaches the point where the two gradients cross. To go further would produce a fear more intense than his desire to reach the goal. To go backward would result in a desire for the goal which is stronger than his fear that he will fail to reach it. As long as the gradients

131

remain where they are, this individual may spend his life within the elliptical circle drawn around the point of intersection (in our example, the boy may dial the first four digits in her phone number and then hang up a hundred times. My example brings back a few memories for me.) The basic emotional experience is anxiety when the obstacle to reaching the goal is fear of failure.

Let me sketch our basic model so far.

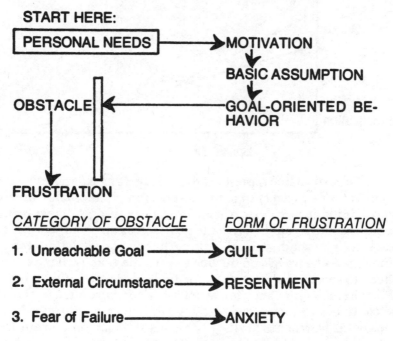

START HERE:

PERSONAL NEEDS ⟶ MOTIVATION
↓
BASIC ASSUMPTION
↓
OBSTACLE ⟵ GOAL-ORIENTED BE-HAVIOR
↓
FRUSTRATION

CATEGORY OF OBSTACLE   *FORM OF FRUSTRATION*

1. Unreachable Goal ⟶ GUILT

2. External Circumstance ⟶ RESENTMENT

3. Fear of Failure ⟶ ANXIETY

Refer to Chart 11 in Appendix

Now let me move on to consider how these three forms of frustration can result in further more complicated personal problems.

I think of guilt, anxiety, and resentment as preneurotic experiences. Full-fledged neurosis occurs when a person develops a symptom or symptom pattern designed to avoid further insult to his self-esteem. The goal of the *preneurotic* is to overcome the obstacle and to reach his fervently desired goal (change wife, live perfectly, make money, etc.). He willingly will evaluate the effectiveness of his goal-oriented behavior and adopt new strategies which hold promise of crossing the barrier and reaching the goal. Although such a response to frustration indicates a healthy flexibility and may avert neurosis, as was discussed in the last chapter, successfully reaching unbiblical goals can never satisfy. The key to maturity lies in choosing the only proper goal for the Christian: knowing God. (For an especially helpful guide to reaching that goal, read Packer's book titled *Knowing God*.)

The neurotic experience is different from the preneurotic. Neurotics no longer are trying to overcome the obstacle. The goal of the *neurotic* is safety. He has tried time and again to reach the goal which he believes is essential to his significance and security. If there has been a long history of successive failure or if he sees no possible way to overcome the obstacle, the frustrated person likely will shift his strategy to a path leading directly to neurosis. Rather than pursuing goals which he believes would provide self-worth, he now begins to direct his efforts toward protecting whatever self-esteem may remain. He gives up the fight to become worthwhile and moves into a holding pattern: hold on to whatever self-esteem you have. Don't try for more — you're asking for more frustration. In the extreme cases where there is no sense of worth at all, the individual retreats into psychosis — a complete break from a painful world. In essence the psychotic is saying, "I've had enough pain. I want no more. I will withdraw entirely into the only safety zone I have — unreality." The difference between neurosis and nonorganic psychosis can be explained most simply in terms of degree of withdrawal.

Many people are, in my terms, living in the preneurotic stage. They are angry with their world (resentment), or they feel down on themselves (guilt), or they live under a cloud of consistent tension and fear (anxiety). They still keep on trying, plodding along in a daily, grudging routine. Christianity is a "grind it out" experience in which these people bravely endure an unhappy life, forcing an occasional "Praise the Lord anyway," and wondering what the joy of the Lord really is.

Underneath this horribly unabundant life lurks some wrong assumptions which have resulted in one of the three problem emotions. The human personality was not designed to operate with guilt, anxiety, or resentment. Either the obstacles will give way to renewed behavioral efforts and the wrong but temporarily satisfying goal will be reached or eventually some form of breakdown will occur. The pathway to neurosis or, in common terms, nervous breakdown is easily traced. At some point after the frustration is great enough or lasts long enough, the individual will stop trying to overcome the obstacle. He will look for a safer existence, away from the painful frustrations of never feeling good or, in my terms, of never experiencing a true sense of worth.

Often there is some precipitating stimulus that triggers the neurotic symptoms. It may seem insignificant: a child not doing what he is told, receiving notice of a bounced check, an apparently trivial snub. The underlying frustration erupts into a desperate and urgent desire to find safety, to get away from more pain of rejection and failure. An everyday experience that is a normal analogue of neurosis is climbing into a hot bathtub to relieve stress. The difference between this normal behavior and neurosis is that the bather intends to emerge from the water into the world of responsibility. The neurotic wants to stay submerged forever.

The flight to safety may include any one of the many classical forms of disorder: phobia, sexual dysfunction, obsessive-compulsive neurosis, tics, etc. A brief illustration may be helpful. A person developed a fear of crossing bridges. Interview material indicated that in order to get to work he had to cross a major bridge. Knowing that symptoms usually are designed to reach the goal of safety, the counselor easily hypothesized that somehow his fear was related to a threat to his self-worth involving his job, a threat he desired to avoid. Questioning with this in mind revealed that the fear developed when the client was given a promotion at work he felt unable to handle. The goal he assumed would provide significance was business success. The obstacle was fear of failure. The frustration therefore took the form of anxiety. At this point the client was preneurotic. He could have solved his problem by admitting his fears and, with the support of friends, tackling the job. Ideally he should have changed his assumption about significance, realizing that success or failure on the job did not, from God's point of view, determine his worth. On the strength of that belief he could then have chosen to accept the responsibility. But the client moved from preneurosis to neurosis when, in an effort to find safety from possible loss of significance through job failure, he unconsciously but purposively attached his fear to bridges. As a result of the crippling fear, he "had to" resign his job and take a lesser, safer position with a firm on the other side of the bridge. He complained that his "crazy fear" cost him his job. But, and this is the point, *that is precisely what he designed it to do.* His fear was not crazy; it was useful as self-protection, a protection totally unnecessary for one who understands the biblical basis for significance and security.

Not all symptoms serve the purpose of reaching safety. Psychosomatic symptoms can be the direct physical result of unhealthy emotional states. The problem emotions of anxiety, resentment, and guilt have physiological correlates which can result over time in real organic problems like ulcers, headaches, or skin conditions. It also is true that these negative emotions can have direct effects on various aspects of behavior such as sexual functioning. Orgasmic dysfunction and impotency, for example, may not always represent an effort to reach safety but may, in fact, be the inevitable physiological result of angry, guilty, or nervous feelings. In many cases, however, it is my opinion that symptoms have a functional significance. That is, they are designed by the client either to overcome the obstacle (preneurosis) or more often to help him avoid further frustration by providing him safety from bumping into the obstacle again (neurosis). We now are in a position to complete the model of how problems develop.

135

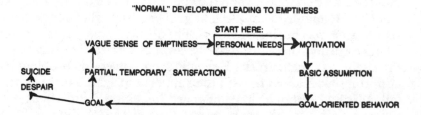

Chart 10 in Appendix

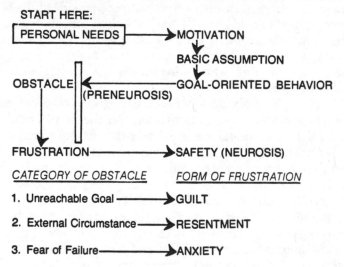

Chart 11 in Appendix

136

CHAPTER 8

What Do You Try to Change?

In order to develop a counseling strategy, we must decide exactly what we are trying to change. Are we trying to change how the client feels? Do we simply try to eliminate his symptoms? Eysenck-type behavior therapists claim that the symptom is the total problem. Eliminate the symptoms and the problem is solved. Most behavior therapy techniques are designed to do just that — modify the symptom behavior. Should we rather be trying to help a person behave more responsibly? Is counseling a matter of laying out a biblical set of behaviors and insisting on conformity? What are we trying to change?

The answer to that question depends on the answer to another question: what are we hoping will result from the changes we produce? In other words, what is our ultimate goal? At this point the reader may want to reread the first chapter. A Christian counselor's goal will differ radically from the goal of the secularist.

Pagan counselors, rooted in humanistic thinking, regard man's individual welfare as supreme. Without objective standards or guidelines for defining what welfare really is, the coun-

137

selor must allow the individual client to determine his own definition of what will make him happy. The ultimate goal for the secularist counselor then is to help his client feel good. Some theorists use fancy language to express their goals but they all reduce to the same thing. Whatever makes the client feel good is desirable unless, most humanists would add, it infringes on the good feelings (welfare) of another. The secularist really is saying that counseling is an effort to help the client achieve whatever he feels will make him happy. Again the Scripture comes to mind, "There is a way which seemeth right unto a man, but the end thereof are the ways of death" (Prov. 14:12).

Christian counselors desire the welfare of their clients too, but they believe that a person's welfare depends on his relationship to Christ. There are absolute standards. A Christian is not willing to help a client feel good in a way which contradicts those absolute standards. Divorcing a disagreeable spouse may make a client feel good, but a Christian believes that the way which *seems so completely right* at the moment and which, in fact, does reduce tension and increase good feelings will lead to personal death (no significance or security) if it contradicts God's directions.

The Christian counselor is in the unique position of advising people to live in a way which may increase the burden of life. A woman client of mine told me recently, "Before I came here, I was involved in a life of sexual fun and games and in a real sense I felt good. It was exciting. Since I have decided to truly commit myself to Christ, I've found that life has become a struggle. The worldly life was easier and happier than the Christian life." And then she added, "But I wouldn't go back for anything. There's no turning around. I've tasted reality. Painful though it sometimes is, I want more. It's what life is all about. For the first time in my life, I feel truly alive, tuned in, I'm together. It hurts like blazes, but it's worth it, because now I'm a person."

If we are clear that we want to introduce changes which will draw a person closer to God whether the immediate feelings are positive or negative, we can evaluate what we should be trying to change.

138

Look back at the finished model at the end of chapter 7. Consider each item in the model to see if (1) it can be changed and (2) changing it will lead us closer to the goal of conformity to the image of Christ. Let's begin with *personal needs*. The need to regard oneself as worthwhile by experiencing significance and security is unalterably a part of the human personality. We can't change anything here.

Motivation, as a generalized drive to meet personal needs, is also a normal, necessary part of personality. We all want to have our needs met and will expend considerable energy to meet them.

My belief should be obvious that the critical change in helping a person live effectively involves altering his Basic Assumption, the third element in this model. *Every problem in the model can be avoided completely if the basic assumption is in line with revealed truth.* The truly well-adjusted person is one who depends on God alone (and what He chooses to provide, which includes the Christian community) to make him significant and secure. Despair, frustration, resentment, anxiety, guilt, a sense of emptiness, neurotic symptoms — every problem can be traced directly to a wrong assumption about how to meet personal needs. The primary problem with people today is misplaced dependency. We depend on everything but God to meet our fundamental needs. What then do we try to change? How a person thinks, what he is depending on, what he believes he must have if he is to feel truly worthwhile. We must change his mind. Transformation depends on renewing not our feelings, not our behavior, not our circumstances, but our minds. Rogers renews feelings. Glasser renews behavior. Skinner renews circumstances. Christ renews minds.

Many counselors neglect this key to true Christian transformation and try to change something else. Some try to change *goal-oriented behavior* from irrational and sinful to rational and biblical. Christians are of course interested in rational, reasonable behavior, but only on the foundation of right thinking. Right behavior without right thinking produces a labored, pressured, effortful brand of Christian obedience. Right behavior springing from right thinking yields a joyful, natural, desired obedience to the God who has made us whole persons, both significant and secure. Even if right behavior accomplishes the goal, if the goal is not biblical, has Christian maturity been promoted? If a woman believes that her entire reason for living depends upon her husband's love, more effective wifely behavior may help her reach the goal of more attention from her husband, but she will not have added an inch to her spiritual stature. Biblical counseling first should teach her that *Christ* is her reason for living (right thinking), *then* should help her become a better wife (right behavior), not primarily to win her husband, but rather to please the Lord and minister to her husband (right goal). If he loves her in return, praise the Lord. She should enjoy his love thoroughly. If her husband does not return her love, she still is a whole, secure woman, capable of going on for God.

Some counselors try to change the *goal*. To meaningfully change the goal, however, requires that a person change his thinking. I told a client recently that she was setting goals which were perhaps unreachable. For example, in disciplining her child, she set the goal of making her child respond properly. But that goal involves an element not totally within my client's control, namely, another human being. I told her that her goal should not be a proper response from her child but rather that she should strive to act responsibly according to biblical principles. Before she could change her goal, however, she needed to change her thinking from "I need my child to turn out right if I am to be worthwhile" to "I am worthwhile as a responsible child of God. I do, of course, want my child to turn out right so I will discipline him in what I understand to be a biblical manner. If my child responds poorly, I will be grieved and will reevaluate my discipline procedures to make sure they are biblical, but I will not be personally threatened because my needs are not at stake. They do not depend on my child's response."

As thinking changes, goals will of course change because goals depend upon the basic assumption about how to meet personal needs. When your thinking is straight and you know that meeting your needs depends only on your relationship to Christ,

140

you are in a position to always set reachable goals. In every situation the broad goal is obedience to Christ. Perhaps that involves responsibly making dinner for your family. Your security does not depend on your family liking your dinner. Compliments are appreciated, of course, but they are *not needed*. Insults are no fun and they do provoke legitimate pain but they are not *personally threatening*. Yet how many women do a slow burn when their husbands complain about dinner. Why? Because at that moment they are depending on their husband's response for their security. The goal of their dinner-making behavior was really to control their husband's response. As I mentioned earlier, efforts to make the best dinner ever to elicit security-building approval is sheer manipulation. It also involves accepting a goal which the wife cannot totally control, which in this case is her husband's response. Whenever a person sets out to achieve a goal which responsible effort does not *guarantee*, he experiences what I call Basic Anxiety. Let a circle represent the limits of what you can achieve if you responsibly choose to work hard within the limits of your ability. If your goals are within the circle, you will not experience Basic Anxiety. There is no fear that the goal cannot be reached. It depends on whether you're willing to put out the effort. But let your goal fall outside the circle. Now your hardest and best efforts do not guarantee the goal. You may reach it. Your husband may smile warmly over a delicious dinner and express love for you but deep inside, underneath the security your husband has given you, is Basic Anxiety: "I need something which I cannot guarantee."

A   B

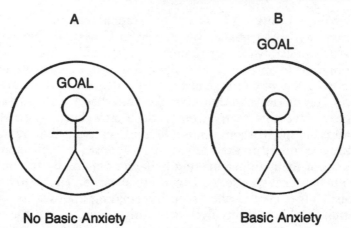

No Basic Anxiety   Basic Anxiety

In Circle A it is possible to behave irresponsibly and not reach appropriate, attainable goals. The result is not anxiety but rather true, nonneurotic guilt. The treatment is exhortation: "Shape up and live responsibly. Your goals are consistent with right thinking. You are secure and significant in Christ. Now He wants you to kiss your wife, play with your kids, witness to your friends, go to work every day. These goals are attainable and appropriate for a Christian. Now do it." In the language of chapter 1, "move over" to the line of obedience. Do what God expects because He already has given you everything you need to live responsibly.

A dramatic example of this was reported in my office recently. A homosexual had come for therapy. He was a Christian and was sincerely desirous of becoming heterosexual but felt completely unattracted to women. In many years of marriage he had never had sexual intercourse with his wife. After we spent a number of sessions rethinking his basic assumptions about his personal needs and learning the biblical basis for adequacy, I said to him, "The time is here. You are now thinking right. Your goal now must be obedience to God. First Corinthians 7 tells me that you are not to deprive your wife of sex. What God commands, He

142

enables you to do. If you will responsibly approach your wife sexually, not with the goal of enjoying it or even performing adequately, you will be living as responsibly as you can. Therefore your assignment for the week is to sexually approach your wife." In our next session he reported with tears in his eyes that he had stepped out on faith (a concept relevant not only to missionary work but also to the bedroom) and God had honored him. For the first time in his life he had behaved heterosexually and he felt like a new man. Had he attempted sex before his thinking had changed, he would have approached the sexual act in an effort to attain significance. The fear of failure would have caused him to avoid it or to function ineffectively. But with changed thinking, he advanced toward the marriage bed not to become significant but because *he already was* — a world of psychological difference. So much for changing goals.

The experience of *guilt* sometimes is the focal point in a counselor's efforts to change things. Bruce Narramore and Bill Counts have written an excellent book on guilt from a Christian perspective. They point out that guilt is a complex emotion not always relieved by simple appeals to the forgiveness of Christ. In my model *false guilt is the result of failing to reach an unreachable goal.* The cure must again involve a change in goals which requires a change in thinking.

Other times counselors may deal directly with *resentment.* "Let it out, express your anger." Or perhaps they will help the client to identify the blocking circumstance responsible for the anger and assist the client to either change or accept the obstacle. Neither approach solves the problem. The real problem again is wrong thinking which led to a wrong goal. If a husband believes he needs a job promotion to be significant, but he is passed over, he likely will resent the company. He may, of course, beat himself over the head for failing but often the emotion of resentment will lurk underneath such self-castigation. His resentment is the product of misplaced dependency.

Anger is sinful if it is a resentful reaction to someone threatening our personal needs. If it is a reaction to a moral wrong in another, anger is righteous and Spirit-produced. Adams in his *Handbook of Christian Counseling* has a useful section on dealing with anger. He points out that there are two wrong reactions to anger: (1) bury it and hold a quiet, perhaps unconscious grudge. Ephesians 4:26 tells us not to let the sun go down upon our wrath. (2) Express it in a lashing out, uncontrolled, attacking way. ("A fool sends forth his spirit," Prov. 29:11, NASB.) Ephesians 5:18 tells us not to be like drunks who squander what God has given ("and be not filled with wine, wherein is squandering or wasting"). To let loose with a violent tirade is a waste of the valuable emotion of anger. Rather, be filled with the Spirit. Use your anger as a motivator to do what you can under God's direction to correct the anger-producing situation. Wife, if your husband really treats you poorly, be angry. Honestly express how you feel but work to become a vehicle which God can use to change him. Your personal goal, however, is not to change your husband. If that is your goal, you will add Basic Anxiety to your problems. Your goal is submission, an entirely reachable goal. Your prayer is that God will reach your husband.

Anxiety sometimes is the factor in our model which therapists try to change. Drug therapy (tranquilizers) and behavior therapy (particularly systematic desensitization) are two direct ways of dealing with anxiety. I have no objection to using either. In my practice, I sometimes desensitize, especially for specific phobic reactions or anxiety-related sexual problems. I also recommend medication on occasions. But a Christian counselor wanting to promote Christian maturity will never stop with that. He will trace the anxiety back to an obstacle en route to a goal determined by wrong thinking, an assumption that something other than God and what He chooses to provide is necessary to meet personal needs.

Neurotic symptoms may be dealt with directly, again with behavior therapy techniques, but a Christian counselor always will look to see if he is helping a client reach safety. If so, he will retrace the reason for the goal of safety and eventually will return to the level of basic assumptions.

Despair and *a vague sense of emptiness* (the remaining elements in the model) may yield somewhat to encouragement, relationship, and support. But a Christian cure will again involve a change in wrong thinking about how to meet needs.

It should be obvious perhaps to the point of labored repetition that reaching the goal of counseling (Over and Up) will involve a change in the client's thinking. What are we trying to change? It is the belief that we need anything other than God and what He chooses to provide to meet our personal needs for significance and security. When that belief is changed and the client is acting upon his new biblical belief, he is on the way to the goal of obedience and maturity.

CHAPTER 9

A Simple Model for Counseling

In chapters 6 and 7 I developed a model explaining how problems develop. Chapter 8 identified the various elements in the model which could be changed and suggested that the core element which must be changed in any truly effective counseling is a person's beliefs about what he needs to become significant and secure. Using the concept developed so far as sort of a mental set, a grid through which to view people, I now want to look in a grossly oversimplified way at what a counselor does during the course of a series of counseling sessions. Perhaps in a later book I will discuss in detail things like how to begin an interview, how to keep conversation running along profitable lines, whether to call a client by his first name, how to handle specific crises like suicide or psychotic breaks, what to do with a very resistant client, when to evangelize, how to handle transference, and so on. These issues are important and can make or break success in counseling. They are of course best taught through modeling and direct supervision. But before they can be dealt with, counselors need a broad strategy for the entire counseling process. This chapter attempts to provide such a strategy.

A Simple Model for Counseling

Before I sketch the seven-stage model I have developed, I first want to discuss the general approach to counseling which to me makes the most sense. Jay Adams has become widely known for his confrontational approach. In his insistence that his model is the only truly biblical one, he argues that the Greek word *noutheteo*, which includes the idea of verbal, directive, instructive confrontation, provides the central concept of Christian counseling. In chapter 1 I referred to Colossians 1:28 where Paul states that he *"nouthetically* confronts" people in an effort to promote their maturity. Although I agree with Adams that Christian maturity is the central goal of biblical counseling, I do not think that the strategy of confrontation exhausts all possible ways to achieve the goal. Certainly there are times when strong firm confrontation is right and necessary. But there are other times when gentle support, encouragement, concerned listening, exploration of inner dynamics, reflection, clarification, and acceptance of feelings are desirable.

A confrontational model is not nearly broad enough to cover all the ingredients of effective Christian counseling. Paul told the Thessalonians to *nouthetically* confront those who were disorderly in their actions, people who were stubbornly resisting their responsibilities. But he also instructed them to comfort people who were despondent or fainthearted. The Greek word for comfort is *paramutheo* and literally means to "speak close." It was used to describe an emotional expression of support and love without a hint of confrontational rebuke. To harshly confront a fainthearted person not only would be cruel but also positively harmful. Paul also advised them to hold strongly onto those who were weak. The thought seems to be that some people need to borrow from another's strength on occasion. Other encouragements to bear each other's burdens support the idea that the local body of believers is to be an interdependent fellowship including confrontation, supportive encouragement, strong assistance, and likely a host of other behaviors. Counseling then includes far more than confrontation and sometimes may not include confrontation at all. John Carter suggests that the word *parakaleo* and its cognate *paraklesis* offer a "much more adequate model of counseling (than *noutheteo)* from a Biblical perspective."[1] He points out that, whereas *noutheteo* and its cognate occur only thirteen times in the New Testament, *parakaleo* or one of its forms is translated (in the King James Version) twenty-nine times as "comfort," twenty-seven times as "exhort," fourteen times as "consolation," and forty-three times as "beseech." He also makes the more important point that *paraklesis* is listed specifically as a gift to the church (Rom. 12:8). Vine says that *parakaleo* denotes "to call to one's side, hence, to call to one's aid. It is used for every kind of calling to a person which is meant to produce a particular effort, hence, with various meanings such as comfort, exhort, desire, call for . . . (and) beseech."[2]

The concept of coming to one's aid in a variety of different ways depending on the problems seems to me to provide a broad and accurate model for counseling, better perhaps than the narrow, more limited approach of confrontation. It is true that my steps in counseling include much opportunity for confrontation, but I would like to think that I approach my clients with the intent not primarily to confront but rather to be by their sides to help. In my efforts to help I engage in a variety of counseling behaviors, including confrontation.

Because I believe counseling includes a wide variety of behavior without one unifying behavioral strategy like confrontation, I do not want to convey in this chapter that my seven-stage model of counseling is a cut-and-dry, mechanical, "ask this, then do that" approach. Far from it. Counseling is relationship. Relationship interactions vary depending on the temperaments, problems, personalities of the people involved. With some you adopt a professional air, with others a relaxed, friendly mood. With some you directively teach, with others you ramblingly explore. With some you assign specific behavioral homework assignments, with others you subtly encourage broad affective or attitudinal changes.

Even though counseling includes a diverse set of operations, still it is possible, I think, to abstract a basic game plan which a counselor, through all his varied behavior, can follow. The rest of this chapter outlines my suggested game plan.

Most people begin a counseling session by discussing either a feeling ("I feel depressed"), an external circumstance ("My marriage is falling apart"), or a problem behavior ("I begin trembling every time I meet someone new"). The initial goal of the counselor is to pinpoint whatever problem emotions exist. If the client begins by sharing a feeling, reflect, draw out, understand, clarify. Try to identify whether the feeling is anxiety, resentment, guilt, despair, or a vague sense of emptiness. Refer again to the model at the end of chapter 7 (chart 11 in Appendix) and you will see that these five emotions include the three primary problem emotions and two other troublesome feelings which people experience. It is my current guess that all other negative emotions are either shadings or derivatives of these basic feelings.

If your client begins by discussing his problem circumstances, ask how he feels about these circumstances. Again the goal is to identify which problem feeling seems to be primary. For example, once you know that your client is boiling with deep resentment, you look for the block to his goal, then define the goal, then examine his goal-oriented behavior, and eventually take a look at the basic assumptions that started the problem sequences.

If the presenting problem is a symptom or a set of problem behaviors, again try to identify what feelings precede or accompany the symptoms. It is important to run through the major areas of life with your client, looking for problem emotions. A simple question like "Tell me about your marriage" can lead to a clear expression of resentment. The areas to cover in initial questioning include occupation, family (marriage, children, parents, siblings), sexual activity, religion and church-related areas, education, and money. In every instance you are looking for problem feelings. The first stage of counseling, then, is: IDENTIFY PROBLEM FEELINGS.

Rogers believes that counseling deals primarily with the affective domain and never really has to leave it. Once a client expresses, understands, and accepts his deepest emotional experiences he will feel together and symptoms will vanish. It is my view that feelings are a necessary initial focus in order to help the counselor trace back to the roots of the problem.

However, once problem feelings are identified, the counselor must move to a consideration of goal-oriented behaviors. The question is "What was my client doing when he experienced the obstacle which created the negative feelings?" Adams helpfully emphasizes that counselors should routinely ask, "What are you doing?" rather than "Why do you feel that way?"

A middle-aged man reported acute anxiety attacks. He reported that the first one occurred while he was filling out an application for a higher paying job. (Incidentally, it often is useful to ask when the client first remembers feeling whatever emotion you have identified in Stage 1. You frequently get a quick and accurate report of the goal-oriented behavior which was blocked.) Further questioning supported the hypothesis that the anxiety attacks occurred whenever some sort of business promotion was involved. It was a simple matter to identify the goal as financial success and the assumption of "significance equals money." Often the analysis is not quite that obvious. But a consistent search for goal-oriented behaviors which when thwarted led to the problem emotion usually will pay off in identification of relevant behavior patterns.

A wife expressed resentment toward her husband (negative feeling). Her resentment was triggered whenever he joked about her appearance. She had for years tried to keep herself attractive (rational goal-oriented behavior) to win his acceptance (goal). He insensitively enjoyed making cracks about some small blemish in her appearance. She began to let herself go in an irrational attempt to have him say, "I love you whether you look good or not" (irrational goal-oriented behavior). Predictably his negative reactions doubled. Just as predictably, she felt a deepening resentment because the frustrating obstacle to her goal was an external circumstance, her husband. Now letting herself go became an expression of her resentment against her husband, but also a

150

neurotic flight toward safety. "If I let myself become dumpy and unkempt, then when he rejects me, I can believe that if I had continued to work at my appearance, he finally would have accepted me."

This entire analysis began with identifying her resentment and then looking for her thwarted goal-oriented behavior. Stage 2, then, is: IDENTIFY GOAL-ORIENTED (PROBLEM) BE- *2* HAVIOR.

Glasser, Mowrer, Szasz in the secular camp and Adams in the Christian camp seem to focus their efforts on changing behavior. Adams in particular compares the behavior pattern (what I am calling goal-oriented behavior) with his understanding of biblical behavior patterns and then commands change. Because he seems to believe that right behavior (obediently doing what God commands) is the single key ingredient for spiritual growth and the antidote for every nonorganically caused personal problem, his approach is to confront the client with his wrong behavior and demand change on the authority of Scripture. As I stated in my first book I believe that obedience is absolutely necessary to effective Christian living. My Over goal in chapter 1 is nothing more than simple obedience. And the *nouthetic* counselors offer excellent material on how to accomplish that goal. But they leave out the "insides" of the behaving person. For me the important part of the "insides" is the person's assumption system and his evaluation of situations based on his assumptions. I therefore believe that after Stage 2, counseling should move inside to an exploration of the person's attitudes and beliefs. *X*

Merely identifying the person's wrong or trouble-producing basic assumption usually is not very difficult. After the negative feelings have been defined, the wrong goal which the person has been pursuing usually is fairly obvious. When you know the goal, you can specify a limited range of possible basic assumptions. If your client has been sacrificing everything (time, health, family) to win a business promotion, then he likely believes that his significance depends upon prestige, or recognition, or perhaps money. As the counselor suggests the various possible assumptions responsible for his selection of goals, the client sometimes will indicate which one fits best by saying something like, "Yeah, that's what I think." It generally is wise for a counselor to zero in as precisely as possible on what the assumption really is. Comments like "I really do feel that way," "Maybe that's it; I'm not sure but it could be," or "That certainly is possible" sometimes are the strongest agreement a client will offer.

A technique developed by Alfred Adler, called the Early Recollection Technique, often is helpful in pinpointing the basic assumption. In this simple procedure you ask your client, "Tell me the earliest thing you can recall, an incident in which you were involved — one day I . . . — finish the sentence." Because the brain stores every event in a huge memory bank, there are literally thousands of events from which the client may select one. This technique is based on the concept that people will remember an event which has special meaning in their psychological make-up. An event is meaningful to the degree that it is relevant to personal needs. Therefore the event that a person recalls should bear some relevance to what he believes is necessary for his sense of self-worth. Details of the recollection often suggest the basic strategy which the person has adopted to reach the goal of personal worth.

Let me illustrate. A middle-aged man, when asked to specify his earliest recollections, came up with the following:

Client: "I recall when I was a little kid about four or five that my dad came home loaded — which wasn't unusual — he was a first-class drunk. He told us he was fired that day and mom hollered and screamed 'You're no good and you never will be.'"

Counselor: "What did you feel?"

Client: "I felt angry, scared, all kinds of things. But I remember I told mom that dad was good, that he would get a job and pay our bills, but he never did."

As an adult this person established a pattern of moving from one job to another. At the first indication that things weren't going well he developed acute anxiety reactions which provided him with a reason to avoid potential failure. His early recollection provided a clue to the explanation for his behavior. From the words of his mother he learned that significance or personal worth depended entirely on job success. From the example of his father he learned to fear the dreadful consequences of failure. His goal-oriented behavior was blocked en route to the goal of success by the fear of failure. The resultant emotion (as explained in chapter 7) was anxiety. Because his anxiety was instrumental in protecting him from what he feared (loss of significance), his anxiety symptoms were useful to him and thereby were reinforced. Direct efforts to reduce the anxiety (systematic desensitization, medication, exhortations to trust the Lord) would have missed the crux of the problem — a wrong basic belief about significance. The early recollection technique was helpful in determining what the problem assumption was. Stage 3 then may simply be called: IDEN- 3 TIFY PROBLEM THINKING.

Once the assumption has been identified, the hard work begins. The next step is to convince the client somehow that his thinking is wrong and to present persuasively the biblical route to meeting personal needs (see my first book for a lengthy discussion of the biblical route). When I first articulated the simple (and rather obvious) concept that my personal needs are fully met by the Lord and what He chooses to provide, I naively and enthusiastically shared my great insight with my clients. When a wife complained that her husband was cold, insensitive, and perhaps was having an affair, I eagerly shared, "Did you know that you don't need your husband to love you? Your need for security can be totally met in a relationship with Christ."

I was chagrined at the burst of apathy with which my grand announcement was met. "Yes, isn't that nice, but I want my husband to love me." Looks of incredulous skepticism, bored yawns, or passive agreement with an insistence that we move on to "important matters" demanded a change in my embarrassingly naive approach. The point is that deeply held assumptions do not easily yield to suggested new ways of thinking.

Social psychologists have written volumes on the subject of attitudes: What is an attitude? How do attitudes develop? Are attitudes primarily affective or cognitive? For the purposes of this chapter let me summarize the opinion of many psychologists by defining an attitude as *a firmly held assumption or belief, usually learned in an emotional climate and therefore charged with strong affective components*. In other words, a person's Basic Assumption that he needs to be financially successful to be significant is more than merely an academic opinion modifiable by contradictory evidence or authoritative instruction. As we might say in everyday language, an attitude is something a person "really believes." Because assumptions are believed emotionally, deep counseling requires far more than simply identifying the wrong assumptions and stating the biblical alternatives.

Let me briefly outline a few suggestions relevant to changing wrong thinking to right thinking.

1. *Identify where the wrong assumption was learned.*

When a client sees that a particular set of circumstances was responsible for teaching him his current belief, the belief becomes less rigid. He is able to see that its source may not be infallible. Discussion of the correctness of his beliefs is easier when the counselor can point out where he learned them.

2. *Encourage expression of emotions surrounding the belief.*

Rather than discussing assumptions about personal worth in a clinical, impersonal manner, the counselor should listen for whatever feelings are associated with the assumption. When a client states, "I need him to treat me better if I am ever to feel loved," the accompanying emotion may be resentment ("He never will") or guilt ("What's wrong with me that no one loves me?"). The sensitive counselor will reflect whatever emotions he picks up as the client's basic assumptions are discussed. As the client feels understood, he will relax and less defensively consider the validity of his thinking.

3. *Support the client as he considers changing his assumptions.*

To give up a long-held assumption is in itself a security-threatening process. Clients know that if they agree with correct thinking the next step is to go back to situations which previously were very painful. Resistance at this point often is the understandable fear of leaving safety. Counselors need to offer encouragement and support. Some therapists speak of "ego borrowing." Paul talks of propping up the weak in 1 Thessalonians 5:14.

4. *Teach the client what to fill his mind with: The "Tape Recorder" Technique.*

I often suggest to patients that they regard their minds as tape recorders. I then have them write out on a three-by-five card their wrong assumption and have them write on another card the contrasting biblical assumption. They are to carry the cards at all times. Whenever they feel upset (guilty, resentful, or anxious), I instruct them to read both cards and to choose to replay at top volume the biblical sentence. The technique admittedly is mechanical but does seem to promote obedience to Paul's injunction to "think on whatever things are true" (Phil. 4:8). Counseling sessions often include discussion about what tape the client was playing.

After the client tentatively grasps the new thinking and can at least recognize the error of his old assumption, Stage 4 is completed. For the sake of a label, Stage 4 might simply be called: CHANGE THE ASSUMPTIONS or perhaps CLARIFY BIBLICAL THINKING.

Stage 5 involves securing a commitment to act on the basis of the newly learned assumption. Playing the right tape is not enough. The client must determine to act consistently with its contents. This step is critical. Because right thinking is fragile at best, behavior change will not flow automatically from the changed thinking. There needs to be a firm, unswerving (if nerve-wracking) commitment: "OK, I agree that this new thinking is biblical. Even if I don't *feel* it, I choose to believe it and commit myself to acting consistently with it even though I do not *feel* like performing the necessary behavior."

Many people get "hung up" right here. When I tell them that they must *do* what is consistent with right thinking whether they feel like it or not, they often say, "But that's hypocritical. I wouldn't mean it. I'd just be pretending." Their point is completely invalid. Certainly their behavior contradicts their feelings, but should subjective feelings be the major guide for a Christian's

155

behavior? We live in a subjective age. "Be true to yourself." "Do whatever you feel." "I've gotta be me." But is such thinking really biblical?

Much of our evangelical Christianity is man-centered. We need to return to a God-centered Christian position which teaches that you do what God says to do whether you feel like it or not. I sometimes *feel* like skipping work. But as I *think* about it, I know I should go to work. What should control my behavior — how I *feel* or what I *think?* I don't always *feel* like obeying God. I often *feel* like sinning. I *know,* however, what is *true* — that God has bought me, that I belong to Him, that He is my Lord. What should control me — how I *feel* or what I *know* to be *true?*

Counseling cannot progress past this point until the client has committed himself (as completely as he can) to behaving consistently with what he has acknowledged to be true *regardless of how he feels.* It is at this point that confession of sin seems most appropriate. Not only wrong behavior (manipulating spouse, sexual sins, losing temper, compromising ethics to make money) should be confessed, but also wrong emotions (holding a grudge against someone for not behaving toward you as you thought you needed) and wrong thinking (believing that God was not adequate to meet your needs).

I recently counseled a wife to draw up a list of everything she resented about her husband. Her wrong assumption was simply that she needed him to love her in order to be secure. Over the years many instances of insensitivity, coldness, and weakness had provoked resentment. I suggested she go through the list, choosing before the Lord to accept every item, to stop resenting him for what he was that he shouldn't be and for what he wasn't that he should be. She also was instructed to acknowledge and confess as sin her resentment against him. When this was done, she was in a position to commit herself to the belief that her husband did not have to be a bit different in order for her to be truly and meaningfully secure. When she committed herself to behaving on that premise, Stage 5 was completed. Perhaps we should call Stage 5: SECURE COMMITMENT.

Stage 6 is the obvious follow-up to Stage 5: plan what your client will do differently now that his thinking has changed. The man who regularly changed jobs at the first sign of impending failure was considering leaving his present job when he came to me for counseling. Armed with his new thinking that significance depended not on job success but rather on responsibly following God's leadership, he committed himself (with a great *increase* in anxiety) to staying with the job. He thought differently, he committed himself to practicing the truth, and then he literally had to behave differently.

The insights achieved in Stages 3 and 4 do not really become a part of the person until he begins acting on them. Christian growth may be defined technically (perhaps a bit mechanically) as the process by which insights understood with the conscious mind seep down into the reflective mind where basic assumptions are deeply held. Progress from merely *assenting* to truth to deeply *agreeing* with truth depends on *behaving consistently with truth*. Paul hints at this idea of two progressive steps in one's grasp of truth when he exhorts Timothy to continue in the things he " . . . has learned" (Step 1) "and has been assured of" (Step 2). We learn many truths but how do we become deeply, unshakably, and experientially convinced of them? Jesus promised that He would make Himself known in a rich, full, personal way to those who knew His teachings and *obeyed* them. "He that hath my commandments, and keepeth them, he it is that loveth me: and he that loveth me shall be loved of my Father, and I will love him, and will manifest myself to him" (John 14:21). His thought seems to be that we can grasp the truth in our conscious mind, stubbornly insisting on its accuracy, but when we act on it (which we will do if we love Him), we will then come to know the truth as a vital, throbbing reality. Jesus Christ, who is the Truth, will make Himself known to us personally in ever-increasing fullness as we continue to behave consistently with the truth we believe. The practice of a truth brings that truth from the realm of abstract, mechanical assertions into the realm of deep conviction and certainty.

157

Let me illustrate. A woman had developed the habitual response of lashing out at people who criticized her. We determined together that her wrong assumption involved the belief that her security depended on always being appreciated for her efforts. Because her temperament was naturally aggressive, she had learned to express through anger the insecurity and hurt occasioned by criticism. We agreed in counseling that the next time she was criticized, she would immediately start playing the biblical tape, "Jesus loves me so I am secure whether I am criticized or not." On the strength of a commitment to act consistently with that sentence, she agreed not to lash back but to respond gently and warmly to her critic. As already mentioned, a standard objection at this point is, "But that would be hypocritical for me to be loving when I feel like knocking his teeth out." The answer is simple: "Yes, it is utterly hypocritical to your *flesh-controlled feelings* but quite consistent with your *Spirit-led beliefs*. If you act consistently with your feelings, you are being hypocritical to your stated beliefs."

She later reported that as she followed the directions, she felt mechanical and unreal, as if she were playing a game. But afterward she began to *feel* a little better about herself. Her day didn't go quite as badly as usual. She even smiled a little at the idea that maybe Jesus' love could become a reality. Her experience was a living illustration of John 14:21 — do what the truth dictates and Christ will slowly become more and more real to you. The order is invariant: first the *facts* (a renewed mind), then the *faith* (doing what the facts suggest), and then the *feelings* (the facts become experientially and subjectively real).

It is interesting to see secular psychologists develop a despiritualized version of this principle. Leon Festinger has written extensively on the theory of cognitive dissonance. He suggests that when two cognitions (beliefs, mental events) are dissonant or in opposition to each other, the one which is reinforced by behavioral consistency will become stronger. In other words over time I will tend to believe more deeply those assumptions which are consistent with the way I behave. Matthew 6:33 teaches that

158

God will supply our material needs if we seek first His righteousness. Two Christians state their agreement with this inspired verse. Five years later the one who has acted on it by giving regularly and generously to the Lord's work is deeply convinced of its accuracy while the other who has given sparingly still claims to believe it but really is not very convinced. The cure for doubt is obedience. Stage 6 involves a delineation of those specific behavioral acts which are consistent with the truth learned in Stages 3 and 4. "If you *need* your husband to stop drinking in order to be secure, you *cannot genuinely* accept him when he drinks. If you do *not* need him to stop drinking, if all that you need for security is the Lord and whatever He chooses to provide in your circle, then you *can* genuinely accept him when he drinks even though you may express your disappointment and deeply desire that he change. This week, whether you smell liquor on his breath or not (but especially if you do), express your concern about his drinking but continue to behave kindly and in an accepting manner. As you do this, you will come to realize more deeply that you can be a secure, well-put-together woman, whether he drinks or not, because you have all that you need in God and what He chooses to provide." Stage 6 might descriptively be labeled: PLAN AND CARRY OUT BIBLICAL BEHAVIOR.

Stage 7 is simply the identification of the lack of sin-related feelings and the presence of "spiritual feelings" (which as I earlier discussed may include many painful emotions). The development of a sense of quietness, togetherness, and peacefulness is a gratifying and reassuring experience. The counselor should look for this evidence of the Spirit's work in his client's life and make sure that it is noticed and enjoyed. Many Christians have had the experience of "feeling really good" when they are consciously abiding in Christ and the experience of feeling that "something is wrong" when they are out of fellowship. Stage 7 reflects upon that wonderful sense of improved adjustment which follows upon a renewed mind (Stage 4), commitment (Stage 5), and obedience (Stage 6) We can call this final stage: IDENTIFY SPIRIT-CONTROLLED FEELINGS.

In diagram form the counseling model developed in this chapter looks like this.

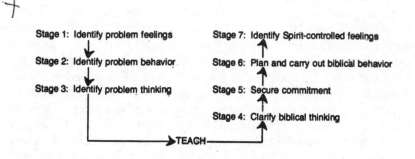

Chart 12 in Appendix

Notes

[1]John Carter. "Adams' Theory of Nouthetic Counseling," *Journal of Psychology and Theology*, vol. 3, no. 3, 1975.
[2]*Expository Dictionary*.

PART IV: DEVELOPING A COUNSELING PROGRAM IN THE LOCAL CHURCH

10. Counseling in the Christian Community

CHAPTER 10

Counseling in the Christian Community

In recent years the increasing demand for counseling services has stimulated serious study of the paraprofessional as counselor. The concept of nonprofessionally trained counselors has caught on with scores of people for whom the idea of "counseling" holds a certain fascination and appeal but who flinch at the prospect of formal schooling. In the churches particularly, group work and peer counseling have spread in epidemic fashion, taking the form of marital encounters, interpersonal sensitivity training, transactional analysis, and the like. Regrettably, many who are drawn to a counseling role are insecure people intrigued by the opportunity for instant intimacy; some are attracted by the apparent position of authority; others find the title "counselor" personally fulfilling. Many people unconsciously are hoping to work out their own hang-ups without exposing themselves in the position of counselee.

With an enthusiasm restrained by some awareness of the problems involved, I envision the development of meaningful counseling within the local church carried on by church members. When it is operating biblically, the body of Christ provides individuals with all the necessary resources to appropriate their significance and security in Christ. But we must not think that opportunities for ministry (which meet significance needs) and fellowship (which meets security needs) automatically will be seized upon eagerly by every believer and clearly understood as relevant to their basic needs. Subtle patterns of sinful behavior and a quietly persistent wrong approach to life will continue to function despite consciously sincere commitment. The heart is deceitful. Wrong beliefs often stubbornly remain until exposed to the clear light of consciousness. Individual counseling often is needed to deal with these kinds of problems. Paul reminded the Thessalonian Christians that he had worked with each one individually in his efforts to guide them toward spiritual maturity (1 Thess. 2:11). The local church must assume responsibility for the individual personal care of each member. Obviously no ministerial staff can deal adequately with the staggering needs for individual attention and concern within the body. Nor should it even try to. The job belongs to the members of the local body.

The counseling model developed in chapter 9 provides a natural basis for defining three levels of counseling which can be integrated gracefully into local church structure.

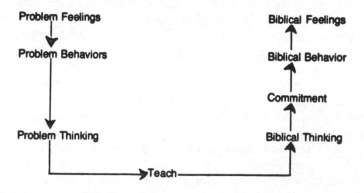

Within this simple but, I believe, comprehensive model three possible levels of counseling can be identified.

Counseling by:

Level I Problem Feelings———ENCOURAGEMENT———▶Biblical Feelings

Level II Problem Behaviors———EXHORTATION———————▶Biblical Behavior

Level III Problem Thinking———ENLIGHTENMENT———————▶Biblical Thinking

Refer to Chart 13 in Appendix

My proposal is this: all members of the body can and should be involved in Level I counseling. Some members of the body (for example, elders, pastors, deacons, Sunday school teachers, other spiritually mature and responsible people) could be trained in Level II counseling. A few selected individuals could be equipped to handle the deeper, more stubborn, complicated problems in Level III counseling. If properly developed, it is my perhaps optimistic but I think realistic hope that every counseling need (except ones which involve organic problems) would be met within the church community.

Level I: Counseling by Encouragement

Have you ever eavesdropped on a conversation between two people waiting for Sunday school class to start?

"Hi, Sally, good to see you."

"Oh, hi, Peggy, how are you?"

"Fine thanks, how are you?"

"Can't complain except that Billy has the flu."

"Is that right? Gee, I hope he's OK. My Susie ran a fever one night last week. Been an awful lot of sickness lately."

"Sure has — oh — here comes Mr. Teldon. Time for class."

Most of us are so used to this kind of conversation that we accept it as normal and we call it Christian fellowship. Yet, inside where no one sees and where we let no one enter, we are hurting badly. Someone in your class is aching about a husband who

165

drinks every night, a daughter who is defiant and probably immoral, a bank account that's dwindling, a job in jeopardy, a marriage on the rocks, a perverted sexual desire which floods the mind with bizarre fantasies during the singing of "Holy, Holy, Holy," or feelings of guilt or emptiness from which death seems welcome relief, and on and on. People in our sin-corrupted world are hurting and hurting badly. Yet so often our interactions within the community of believers, people with whom we share the profound oneness of common membership in Christ's body, are casually friendly, genuine but shallow, and utterly trivial. We warmly shake hands every Sunday with people who are about to come apart at the seams and we never know it until they do.

The majority of people who are experiencing personal anguish can be tremendously helped by the warm, genuine interest of people who care. When I feel loved, my burdens seem lighter. The knowledge that I am loved provides me with strength to face my problems and better enables me to believe in a loving Lord. A loving body gives me a perfectly legitimate sense of security as I meditate on the marvelous truth of my oneness with other believers, made possible by Jesus' supreme act of love. The reality of the family I have in Christ indelibly impresses itself on me. I recently spoke to a singles group, people who were divorced or never married. Their greatest problem, they indicated, was loneliness: no one to share life with, no family. As I discussed their situation, I felt rather like a male obstetrician telling a woman what it was like to have a baby: I have observed the phenomena often but I've never experienced it. Yet the concept I shared is biblical and therefore valid, regardless of my lack of experience in the adult single life. The concept is this: the only eternal family is the family of Christ; our natural families through birth or marriage are temporary and illustrative. Our heavenly family (which exists right now) is eternal and deeply substantive. We need to practice that truth in our local churches in many ways, including mutual loving support. This is Level I counseling. Counseling by Encouragement depends upon an awareness of painful emotions in a member of the family and a sincere effort to understand them, growing out of an attitude of compassion and concern for the person who hurts.

Perhaps the Level I counselor gains initial awareness of the problem by noticing that his brother or sister is quieter than usual, a little distant or strained in his conversation, perhaps gloomy, or maybe indefinably but obviously different than usual. Prompted by compassion and by a desire to communicate the love of Christ, he then would look for an opportunity to encourage, to engage in meaningful conversation with the objective of helping the other. I might mention quickly an important caution: be careful that you don't become a syrupy, "Let me lovingly lick your wounds whether you're injured or not" type. Nothing at all is wrong with friendly, surface chitchat, provided you are capable of shifting to a more intensely personal level if required by the situation. No one is more offensive to me than a well-meaning would-be counselor looking for a despairing victim. I am not suggesting that we *create* counseling opportunities, but rather that we sensitize ourselves to those valid ones which cross our paths.

While on the subject of caution, let me offer another suggestion. Some people are sympathy grabbers, often unintentionally, but they are still anxious to be noticed. A down look, a depressed tone, a grave, heroic shrug of the shoulders and a stalwart if somewhat burdened smile — these maneuvers often are designed to attract sympathy. I get thoroughly disgusted when I catch myself praying publicly in tones designed to communicate spiritual depth and theological brilliance rather than simply expressing myself to my Father. If you think you've never been guilty of so childish a ploy, I am tempted to gently recommend a somewhat more sensitive self-analysis. We all love to produce an effect, create an impression, stir up favorable attention. Level I counselors should take care to watch for those who seem consistently to demand attention by rehearsing their concerns either openly or subtly, without making responsible efforts to deal with their problems. Such folks need less encouragement and more exhortation (Level II counseling).

With these cautions in mind let me go on to illustrate how Level I counseling might operate. Assume that you notice a friend looking a bit blue during Sunday school class. You have no clear idea about what circumstances might be weighing him down. Remember that what looks to you like a sad countenance may in fact be the observable expression of a bad case of heartburn from too much coffee at breakfast. Perhaps your first response to the situation would be a simple prayer: "Lord, if you desire to use me in his life as an encouraging brother, I am willing. Make me sensitive without becoming rudely intrusive." Wouldn't it be something if Christians were routinely looking for opportunities to encourage? Half the battle in developing Level I counseling in the local church is to stimulate a continuous attitude of helpfulness in each member toward one another.

Returning to our example, after class is over you make your way to your friend and offer a warm, casual greeting.

"Good to see you. How're things going for you?" Don't begin with "You look down, what's the matter?" unless you know the person well and can be relatively assured that he would welcome your personal inquiry. If the initial question is motivated by genuine interest and love rather than by "busybodiness" or mere courtesy, the response is likely to contain some indication of a problem *if indeed there is one*. Again, the real problem may best be handled with a tablet of Alka-Seltzer.

Perhaps your would-be "client" responds with "This isn't one of my better days but I'll be fine, how are you?" Suppose you think you notice a mood of discouragement in his voice and manner. What does a Level I counselor say at this point? Think what *you* would say. Remember, all you are trying to do is to understand and express love, to reinforce the liberating truth that the love of Christ is fully sufficient to meet one's need for security. The following responses are typical examples of what *not* to say.

1. "Well, we all have days like that." This response effectively ends the conversation by not taking the person seriously enough to avoid meaningless clichés.

168

2. "Isn't it great to know that all things work together for good?" Spiritual truths offered glibly as an instant panacea have the effect of driving painful feelings underground where they remain unresolved and frequently produce psychological problems ("If all things work for good then I should not be upset; I'll pretend I'm not").

3. "Hope things get better. I'm sure they will." No interest in the person is communicated. Christian hope is presented as empty well-wishing utterly devoid of foundational content.

4. "What's wrong?" If you know the person well, this may be a good response, but even then it probably is too direct. Most people are not ready to reveal significant conflicts quickly. A direct question like this may frighten the person into retreating with a surface answer like, "Oh, nothing really, at least nothing that a good dinner won't cure."

5. "Business not going too well?" Before you know where the problem lies, introducing a specific possible area of conflict is no more than guesswork and tends to make you appear insensitive. Even if you had reason to believe the concern involved his business, it is better to give him an opportunity to specify the exact conflict.

Level I counselors must never offer "canned" responses. Beginning counselors often handle their nervousness by hiding behind a set of clever, appropriate phrases or sentences. I once told a practicum student to begin his response to a client with the words "You feel . . ." in order to develop in the counselor the mental set of empathy. In his next taped session he began *every* sentence with those "therapeutic words" whether they fit or not. The client at one point asked, "What time is it?" He dutifully responded, "You feel curious about the time." Nothing ruins counseling more quickly than a contradiction of naturalness through the use of artificial, forced, programed interactional technique. A counselor must, even when using a structured behavior therapy technique like systematic desensitization, be himself. The few suggested sentences below are intended only to point the reader in a broadly appropriate direction. Your words must be your own.

Responses like the following might convey the attitude, "I'm here, I'm listening, I care."

"Sounds like you're a little down."

"Not feeling as good as you'd like, huh?"

"You feel a little weighted down today."

If your "client" finds even these mild responses too threatening (and some will — these reflections may be dipping into a large reservoir of painful emotions), he may back away by denying his feeling. "Naw, I don't feel all that bad." Again, consider the possibility that perhaps he really doesn't feel all that bad in which case you lose a client and gain a relaxed encounter of light fellowship. Either he isn't hurting badly and doesn't need your ministrations, in which case no harm has been done and in fact something positive has perhaps happened (presenting yourself as a caring brother may provide opportunities to help at a later date), or he would love to unburden himself to someone but at this moment does not feel safe enough to do so. Again, establishing yourself as a caring person may result in his seeking you out next Sunday, hoping to share his burdens with you at that time.

If the person opens up, your responsibility remains basically unchanged: communicate interest and concern. So many people wonder, "What can I say to help? I'm no counselor." Others feel pressured to solve the problem on the spot. Level I counseling offers the powerful ingredient of true acceptance. In earlier chapters I developed the idea that so many problems result from a frustrated security need, a deeply felt attitude that "no one cares about me." Don't think of Level I counseling as *merely* communicating love. There is nothing "mere" about truly accepting another human being. Continuing to warmly reflect and involve yourself in whatever emotional pain your fellow Christian shares will in itself have a powerful and sometimes revolutionary effect. Don't quickly offer advice or suggest referral. Stay awhile and listen. If good advice occurs to you, offer it. If referral to another source of help seems appropriate, do it. In many cases your acceptance of the hurting individual will provide the foundation upon which he will be able to resolve successfully whatever problems he is experiencing.

The following represents an example of an effective attempt to counsel at this level. Two women are having lunch.

Hazel: "Cathy, I sometimes get so frustrated with George. Submitting to him is not easy."

Cathy: (I'd like to ask what's wrong but I'll just let her know I hear her and see if she wants to tell me. Maybe I can help by just being a good listener.)
"Sounds like you're having a pretty rough time."

Hazel: "Oh, Cathy, he just will not face up to the problem we're having with our son Peter. Peter is skipping school, sassing me all the time. I'm convinced he's on drugs and George refuses even to talk about it."

Cathy: (I'd like to agree with her about how bad George is — he sure sounds like he's falling down on the job — but that might increase her resentment. She is having a tough time though.)
"He just won't face up to it, huh? That must be frustrating."

Hazel: "It really is. How far do you carry submission anyhow? Do I have to watch my son go down the drain until George decides to act?"

Cathy: (That is a tough question. I'd like to tell her to rip into her husband but that doesn't seem biblical. I really don't know what she should do. Maybe I can encourage her by letting her know I share some of her confusion.)
"That's puzzling to me, too. It's hard to understand exactly what God would have us do sometimes."

Hazel: "I mean, it's so bad that the only time George even talks to Pete is when he hollers at him. I can't stand it. He makes me so angry."

171

Cathy: (Oh, oh. She is really resentful and ready to blow up. I'd better help her see that she is feeling pretty bitter.) "Hazel, as I hear you talk, I'm confused about what you should do. But it does sound like you're getting pretty bitter at George."

Hazel: "Yes, I guess I am. But wouldn't you?"

Cathy: (Now she's trying to justify her bitterness. If I help her see what she's doing maybe she'll deal with it.) "Hazel, could it be you're feeling a little guilty about getting so resentful and are trying now to say that you're justified in being bitter?"

Hazel: "I guess so but it's just so hard."

Cathy: (This is no time for rebuke. She needs to deal with her anger and to better understand submission, but I'm not sure if I have the answers. I'll refer her to a Level II counselor in our local body. For now I'll lend her the loving acceptance she deeply needs to get through this.) "It must be harder than I can ever imagine. Hazel, I really am concerned about how difficult things are; you must be aching inside. Maybe you need to see exactly how Scripture teaches you to handle situations like this. Why don't you let me call Phil Kearney at the church and arrange for him to talk with you. He does a lot of talking with people in our church about how to handle difficult situations like yours biblically."

Often Counseling by Encouragement will provide the strength necessary to do what obviously is right. On some occasions, as in the example above, Counseling by Exhortation might be required. If Cathy felt comfortable in shifting to Level II, she could have dealt with the problem herself. If she really was not sure of what biblical behavior would be, then referral to a more knowledgeable Level II counselor would be appropriate.

Level II: Counseling by Exhortation

The Book of Judges ends with a sentence that explains the many problems the Israelites were experiencing: "Every man did that which was right in his own eyes" (Judges 21:25). Now it is important to notice that these people really thought the way they were handling their problems was right. The Lord's commentary on their behavior was, "The children of Israel did evil again in the sight of the LORD" (Judges 13:1). They earnestly believed they were right. God declared them to be evil.

So often people respond to a problem circumstance in a way which to them makes sense. Because the heart is deceitful, it is possible to be consciously sincere and yet utterly wrong. Rogers teaches that the infallible guide to productive, integrative behavior is one's own set of "visceral organismic valuations." In simpler language, Rogers advises people to do what is right in their own eyes, to trust their deepest internal "gut" reactions as a valid compass for charting their behavioral course. If you feel it, do it! How thoroughly unbiblical! Christians must not place final trust in experience of any sort but rather in the propositional revelation of Scripture. A professing Christian client of mine was debating whether he should leave his wife. Our conversation went like this.

> *Client:* "I really don't know how I feel about it. Maybe I should leave her; maybe I'd be happier, I just don't know."
>
> *Counselor:* "You sound pretty confused about your feelings. What is your understanding of what God is telling you to do?"
>
> *Client:* "That's hard to figure. Sometimes I feel He is telling me 'Why stay miserable, get out and enjoy a little bit of life,' and then other times I don't know."
>
> *Counselor:* "God has spoken clearly on the subject in the Bible. He tells you not to break what He has joined. He forbids divorce except on grounds of

173

adultery and desertion and you have neither
ground."

Client: "But I just don't know how I feel."

Counselor: "Don't you see that as a Christian how you feel is
not really relevant to your decision? God has told
you what He wants you to do. The only issue is
whether you choose to obey God or not. If you
choose to obey Him, then I'll work at helping you
behave biblically toward your wife and your feelings will come along."

Client: (in a loud burst of anger) "Wait a minute. Why
should I do what a book written 2000 years ago
tells me to do?"

His reaction is rather typical, I would judge, of many
people's attitude toward the Scriptures. Francis Schaeffer has
expressed the opinion that our major battleground today *within
evangelical circles* involves the authority of Scripture. Biblical counseling must be precisely that — biblical. We need authoritative
direction in dealing with the abundant and confusing com-
plexities that present themselves every day. When we face a
problem situation and must determine a course of action, we can
turn for help in several directions. (1) "Expert advice" is available. The experts in family living and problem solving who sometimes are struggling unsuccessfully with their own concerns often
disagree with one another. More importantly, their advice is
suspect on the grounds that it can never be more than the opinion
of fallible people. (2) "Common sense" may be the guide, but the
collection of obvious, intuitive wisdom labeled "common sense"
again represents nothing more than the opinions of error-prone
people. (3) We can blindly trust our "inner judgment," hoping
that our urge to live effectively blended with a basic sense of
wisdom will combine to lead us along productive, peaceful paths.
Once more, the obvious comment must be made: to follow your
own hunches or "instincts" is to trust a biased, limited, fallible,
fallen human being. The point is clear. Any guideline other than
God's Word is suspect. Christians have the tremendous opportu-

nity to build their lives according to a guaranteed program. Level II counseling essentially consists of the specification of a scriptural strategy for handling a given situation.

Anyone who has attempted to communicate biblical advice to unhappy people has noticed with chagrin that many folks stubbornly balk at scriptural directives. A woman came to see me, complaining about her alcoholic husband. (Let me again state that I am never referring to whomever comes to mind as you read my case descriptions. Each case I report is disguised enough to prevent recognition.) For years she had been trying to get him to change, running through every technique and feminine wile her ingenuity could conceive. When this woman came to see me, she wanted to leave him. As I looked at her — bitter, depressed, despairing, utterly miserable — I thought of Peter's inspired advice that wives should submit to their unbelieving husbands. Then I thought of the psalmist's expression of love for God's words: "How sweet are thy words unto my taste! yea, sweeter than honey to my mouth" (Ps. 119:103). I couldn't imagine that if I were to read to this woman God's words through Peter, "Wives be in submission to your husbands," that she would respond with "Oh, what a sweet, marvelous idea. I so appreciate this wonderful advice. I am eager to accept that drunk stretched out on the sofa at home." How then can biblical advice be regarded as sweet? Let me illustrate.

Some time ago I purchased a Rumbler for my boy. For those of you who don't know, a Rumbler is a sporty, fancy, riding vehicle for young children. My son showed me the picture in the paper and I agreed to buy him one. When I went to the store, they gave me not what I had seen in the newspaper ad, but a large cardboard box which, I later found out when I emptied the contents on our garage floor, contained what appeared to be about 10,000 separate parts. In the midst of this confusing array I spied a booklet with the delightfully deceptive title "Easy Assembly Steps." I thumbed through the nine pages and the fifty-four easy steps, each instructing me to join a part which I had never heard of and couldn't find with another part which I had never heard of and couldn't find. You must understand that I have not been blessed with mechanical ability. When our washing machine breaks, I lay my hands on it and pray, then call the repairman. Standing there in my garage contemplating the huge pile of assorted metal, rubber, and plastic, and holding an instruction book designed for graduate engineers, I felt lost, alone, and entirely unmotivated. And then my boy arrived home from school. He popped his head in with a big grin and said, "Hey, dad, did you get my Rumbler?" Then he saw the pile. As he sized up the predicament, his smile vanished and he said "Oh" in an understanding, resigned sort of way, and slowly left.

I love my boys. Nothing thrills me more than to see them happy. I thought about the instruction book and realized that it really was not my enemy but my friend. By following what it said I could produce something that would please my child. It wasn't easy to understand or to follow, but now I was motivated. Each of the fifty-four steps became like honey in my mouth as I thought about the pleasure which figuring them out and following them would bring to my son. Two days and much frustration later I presented a snazzy, well-built Rumbler to my ecstatic boy.

Is my point clear? The Bible is our instruction book. Our lives often are in 10,000 pieces, scattered in disarray with little direction or pattern. The rule book, the Bible, is not always easy to understand and sometimes very difficult to follow. We often have to call in specialists to help us interpret what it means. God anticipated this need and gave to the local church the gift of teachers. My vision includes training some of these teachers in Level II counseling, equipping them to specify clearly whatever steps are needed to bring order into disorderly lives. Motivation to follow the rule book is singular: I want to please the Lord. I love Him. He died for me. As I carefully heed the directions in the Bible, my life will become a source of delight to Him. Only within this perspective can biblical directions *always* be regarded as sweet, as honey to my mouth.

Above all else Level II counseling requires a knowledge of the Bible. Counseling technique is important. An ability to establish rapport, to reflect feelings accurately (Level I) and to react sensitively to a person's needs are critical. But without a working knowledge of biblical principles of living a person simply cannot counsel at Level II.

Bill Gothard in his seminars and Jay Adams in his books offer a most helpful and comprehensive statement of many biblical principles for dealing with problem situations. Training at Level II would include a review of many situations and a discussion of applicable biblical principles like those taught by Gothard and Adams. For example, a Level II counselor would be able to think through a situation like this. Mr. A has committed adultery. His wife doesn't know about it. He tells you that she would leave him if she found out. He has repented of his sin and wants to improve communication with his wife. What do you tell him to do? Should he tell his wife? Are there biblical principles which apply? Or are we dependent in this situation on sanctified common sense?

A teen-age girl's dad is a deacon in the church. She comes to the pastor and confides in him that her dad and mother are having serious marital problems. What should the pastor do? The daughter doesn't want her parents to know she shared their private battles with the pastor but she was so worried she wanted help. Should the pastor break her confidence? Ignore the situation? Have lunch with her dad and gingerly and discreetly broach the subject with him?

Examples like these should indicate that more is required of a truly effective Level II counselor than a concise list of well-defined principles. He needs to be able to "think biblically." In addition to a knowledge of basic biblical principles of marriage, communication, handling anger, raising children, sexual behavior, divorce, addiction, dealing with temptation, etc., he must "let the word of Christ *dwell . . . richly* in all wisdom" (Col. 3:16). He must be facile in thinking through complex situations and discerning the approach which would be the most consistent with biblical teaching. Before Paul offers a few specific principles of living in Colossians 3:18-22, he instructs his readers to do all in the name of the Lord Jesus (Col. 3:17). He then goes on to offer examples of such behavior and then repeats again, "Whatsoever ye do, do it heartily, as to the Lord" (Col. 3:23).

Candidates for training in Level II Counseling then would be Christians who have a broad familiarity with Scripture and are actively expanding it through study. Training would focus on (1) basic principles of Christian living in several key areas, (2) how to think through a problem situation and arrive at a biblical strategy for dealing with it and (3) general interviewing skills. Pastors and other church leaders are obvious prospects for such training.

Let me offer a brief and condensed illustration of Level II counseling. In our example of Level I counseling Cathy had referred Hazel to Phil, a man in the church recognized as a Level II counselor.

> *Phil:* "Hazel, Cathy told me about your situation. I can understand your perplexity. It's a painful problem, I'm sure."
>
> *Hazel:* "I really don't know what to do about it."
>
> *Phil:* "Tell me the problem as you see it, just to make sure I have it right."

Hazel reviews the situation involving a son on drugs with whom she has little communication and a husband who refuses to deal with the situation.

> *Phil:* "What sort of approach have you tried in dealing with this?"
>
> *Hazel:* "There's nothing I can do."
>
> *Phil:* "Hazel, even though I'm sure you feel terribly locked in, the beauty of Scripture is that there is a biblical way to deal with every situation. The results might not always be what you want but you can have a deep peace and a knowledge that your behavior is pleasing to God and that He is working through you to accomplish His purposes. I can guarantee you that peace and knowledge."
>
> *Hazel:* "All I care about is that my son turns out OK."

178

(Hazel is subject to Basic Anxiety, assuming responsibility for something she can't control. Whatever blocks her goal of making her son turn out right will elicit resentment. No wonder she's so angry at her husband. She sees him as the obstacle to straightening out the boy.)

Phil: "That's pretty normal and understandable, Hazel, but your attitude isn't biblical. You cannot totally control how your son turns out. It's true you can have a great deal to do with it, but you cannot control it."

Hazel: "Well, is it wrong to want my boy to be a good Christian?"

Phil: (Oh, oh — she's a little hostile. I don't want to turn her off unnecessarily, but I must get her to see that she has the wrong goal.)
"Of course not, and I want to do everything I can to help you with your son. My concern, though, is with your goals. A Christian's goal must in every situation be, 'Lord, what can I do to please You?' It seems to me your goal is, 'What can I do to change my son?' Can you see that?"

Hazel: "Yes, I guess so."

Phil: "Good. Suppose your goal were simply to please the Lord in how you respond to your son and to your husband. What do you think you could do that would honor the Lord?"

Hazel: "Well, for starters, I guess I shouldn't nag my husband about it."

Phil: "It's tempting to nag, isn't it? But you're right. Peter tells wives that they are to have a meek and a quiet spirit. Do you know what that means?"

Hazel: "Be a doormat I guess."

Phil: "C'mon Hazel (said patiently with a smile), can you picture God wanting you to be a doormat? What it means is that you are to display the peace of knowing that God is in control of things."

179

Hazel: "But shouldn't I speak up at all? I'm letting an evil continue unchecked if I say nothing."

Phil: "By all means say something. Christians should take a strong stand against evil, but their stand must never violate biblical directions. Tell George exactly how you feel but with an attitude not of 'I'm so angry at you for ignoring this' but rather of 'I need to share this with you. It concerns me deeply but I know God has His hand on things.' "

Hazel: "That won't work."

Phil: "It depends on what you mean by work. Will it glorify God? Yes. If that's your goal, then this plan will work. But you're right, it might not change George. Let's take a look at other areas of your marriage to see how well you're going about this business of really accepting him and conveying to him an attitude of loving respect."

Counseling then would explore such things as her housekeeping habits, her sex life with George, her way of greeting him when he comes home — anything that might contradict her responsibilities as a wife. Her approach to dealing with her son would need to be explored. If her husband continued in his obstinate refusal to deal with the situation, the counselor would recommend (1) that she express her concern but accept her husband by treating him well, (2) that she deal firmly with her son. When Moses did not assume his responsibility as a father, Zipporah stepped into the gap and circumcised their child. God apparently honored her behavior by not punishing Moses as He intended. Scripture also teaches that parents have a responsibility to discipline children. For a woman to sit idly by while her husband fails to follow Scripture would involve her in disobedience. Biblical submission to a husband never includes engaging in a behavior pattern which sinfully contradicts other biblical principles.

Level II counseling sometimes will be ineffective. Many people report, "I know what I should do but I just can't do it." Authoritarian insistence that they can do it may provoke further resistance, frustration, and sometimes deep despair. I recently worked with a godly woman who apparently could not control her temper. She was familiar with how a Christian should deal with anger but found herself fighting a losing battle. Years of praying for help had resulted in minimal progress. Her faith was giving way, yet she was clinging desperately to the certainty that God loved her and had a plan for her life which His power would enable her to follow. But how to lay hold of the power? In this instance Level III counseling was required. A few months of thinking through her basic assumption about security and of understanding how her family was an obstacle to reaching what she wrongly believed she needed in order to be secure provided her with a rational plan for solving her problem. A counseling approach based on the ideas presented in this book helped her to appropriate the marvelous truth that her security already was established in Christ. As she came to see that she did not *need* her family to be different in order to be secure, she was able to accept them and to stop resenting them. Her temper problem was resolved as her resentment disappeared.

Since most of this book has dealt with a model for Level III counseling, in this chapter I will deal with it only briefly.

Level III: Counseling by Enlightenment

To be a Level III counselor requires more than a few weekends of training. It is my guess (and I intend to test my speculation in a training program) that a minimum of six months and a maximum of one year with weekly two-and-one-half to three-hour classes would be enough to provide a mature Christian with the necessary knowledge and experience to function independently as a Level III counselor.

After identifying and empathizing with a person's problem feelings (Level I) and after assessing what behavioral patterns violate biblical principles (Level II), a Level III counselor will look underneath the wrong behaviors into the thought world, expecting to find wrong assumptions about how to become significant and secure. These erroneous beliefs are the culprit. They have produced the wrong behaviors which have in turn produced the wrong feelings. Scripture emphasizes over and over that the thought world, what a person thinks and believes, is central to his functioning. If we are to profoundly change how a person functions, we must help him change what he believes. The revolutionary change of becoming alive to God in the new birth depends upon a changed belief. When I *understand with my mind* that I am a lost sinner, helpless, without hope, deserving a holy God's righteous punishment, when I *understand with my mind* that Jesus is God, that He led a sinless life, that when He died on the cross He was enduring in my place the punishment I deserved, when I *understand with my mind* that God will give me the gift of life with Himself, eternal life, if I trust in what Jesus did for me and not in what I do for myself, then, when I believe in the Lord Jesus Christ, I shall be saved (Acts 16:31). Commitment to Christ depends upon some level of *understanding* of the gospel. Then, because I am justified and, as a seal of my new life, the Holy Spirit comes to dwell within me to help me understand more truth about Christ ("He will lead you into all truth," "You shall know the truth and the truth shall make you free") so that I can become more like Him.

I am transformed by the renewing of my mind. As I grasp *with my mind* that my needs (significance and security) are fully met in Christ, then I am enabled to better conform my behavior patterns to Christ's example and to enjoy the deep peace of a growing maturity. Both justification, the once for all judicial declaration by God that I now am regarded as righteous, and sanctification, the process by which my character becomes more like Christ's, revolve around the content of my mind. God's work is to enlighten the unregenerate mind and to continue enlightening the regenerate mind. The Christian counselor's work is to function as an instrument through which the Holy Spirit enlightens minds regarding the truth of significance and security in Christ. And that is what Level III counseling entails — probing deeply into the hidden parts of the mind where people hold tenaciously to certain assumptions, exposing those beliefs which deny the sufficiency of Christ to meet our personal needs of significance and security, teaching that Christ is sufficient, and then encouraging new behaviors in the truth that our needs are met in Christ.

The counseling process follows the model presented in chapter 9: (1) empathize with painful feelings, (2) identify sinful behavior patterns responsible for the negative emotions, (3) uncover the wrong thinking which led to the maladaptive behavior, (4) enlighten the individual to biblical thinking about personal needs, (5) secure a commitment to behaving consistently with truth, (6) plan behavioral changes which reflect that commitment, and (7) enjoy the ensuing feelings of love, joy, and peace.

In an effort to clarify the actual conversation involved in going through these steps, let's return to Hazel's dilemma. Suppose after five sessions of Level II counseling she still was worried about her son Peter, angry with her husband George for his seeming indifference, and found it next to impossible to keep quiet about George's lack of intervention as a father. In her fifth session with Phil she reports that she is speaking softly to George, making him nice dinners, greeting him at the door with a kiss, expressing herself gently about the problem with Peter, in short, following all the homework assignments Phil had given her. But still she is boiling inside, choking her anger and forcing nice words to come out of her mouth when addressing her husband. When she sees Peter, all she can do is worry. She has tried to deal with him firmly according to the counselor's suggestions, but feels on the inside like a seething volcano about to erupt. Tranquilizers, prayer, memorizing Scripture, telling a friend, rebuking the devil have all been tried. What next?

Those who deny the need for a deeper level of counseling would perhaps wag their heads sadly and pray that Hazel would deal with her stubborn rebellion. Poor Hazel. She thought she had dealt with it. She had confessed it as sin and prayed for help. What else could she do? At this point she may become convinced she is mentally ill, or she might become rather fed up with God, or perhaps she might seek help from a secular professional, undoubtedly with guilt that she couldn't go God's way. In my thinking, Hazel should not be written off as a stubborn reprobate until she has been exposed to Level III counseling. Now please understand my thinking. She may indeed be an utterly stubborn rebel, locked by her sinful will into a pattern of disbelief and disobedience. But her counselor is in no position to decide that until he has probed her thinking about security, uncovering whatever wrong thinking might be there and enlightening her (Level III) concerning the truth of security in Christ. If she still refuses to behave in faith on the *conscious understanding* that her needs are met in the Lord, at some point the counselor would be justified in regarding her as sinfully unwilling to believe God.

Suppose Phil had told her that her problems were perhaps a bit more complicated than he was equipped to handle and then made arrangements for her to see a Level III counselor in the church. If Hazel had refused to cooperate with Phil in his instructions to handle her problems biblically, referral would be inappropriate. Deeper counseling is no cure for lack of cooperation, but it sometimes is a cure for lack of success with a cooperating client.

A Level III counseling session might go like this. We'll pick up the session after they have reviewed where things stand.

Counselor: (My first step is to identify clearly the problem emotions. I am looking for anxiety, resentment, guilt, vague emptiness, or despair. Seems pretty clear that Hazel is resentful about George and anxious about Peter, so I'll openly suggest that.)

"Hazel, you're still feeling pretty angry with George and upset and worried about Pete."

Hazel: "And I've tried so hard to do what Phil said. I really have, but it didn't help. I feel like such a failure."

Counselor: (Her frustration sounds less like self-pity and more like a realistic response to what has happened in counseling so far. She needs support and hope.)

"Hazel, I know you have tried hard. Phil told

184

me you were most cooperative. I wouldn't have agreed to see you if you hadn't done everything Phil said. Sometimes just doing right isn't enough to change things. When this happens, it usually means that we have to probe a little deeper to find and correct the real problem. That's what we'll be doing together."

Hazel: "Please don't give me more assignments. All I do is get frustrated."

Counselor: (At this point I can accept her frustration as realistic and not rebellious, so I'll simply be understanding and move the conversation toward a consideration of her security needs. I can assume that because she is a woman I probably am dealing with unmet security needs. Let me move in that direction.)

"Don't worry. No more assignments for now. I'm more interested in what you are thinking when you feel so angry with George. Suppose he were dealing with Peter as you want him to. Why do you suppose that would make you feel good? How would you evaluate things then?"

(Here I'm looking for the goal which she believes will bring her security.)

Hazel: "I feel so alone in dealing with Peter. I really can't handle him. I would feel so much better if I knew I had some help."

Counselor: "So your goal is to have a strong person assist you with a difficult responsibility. You feel that without help you might make a real mess of things."

Hazel: "Yes, I guess I do feel that way."

Counselor: "Making a mess of things would be bad."

Hazel: "Yes, of course — my son is at stake. I don't want to see him ruined."

Counselor: "But Phil explained to you and you accepted the idea that you must assume responsibility only for

185

what you can control and then believe that God is in charge of the rest. If you do believe that, then your emotions about your son's welfare should be deep sorrow and motivated concern to do all that God tells you to do. And you've done all that. Yet you're still anxious. That tells me that more must be involved than a concern for your son's welfare."

Hazel: "I can't imagine what."

Counselor: "Hazel, let me ask you an apparently unrelated question. Think back to your childhood. What's the earliest incident in your life you can recall? Y'know, 'One day I . . .' — can you finish with an incident from years ago?"

Hazel: "As far back as I can recall? Let's see. Well, I can remember once that mother asked me to help her with getting the house ready for company. I must have been five or six years old. She told me to clean the bathroom."

Counselor: (I wonder if her security depends upon performing up to other people's standards. Maybe she feels her security depends on performing as a good mother and her performance is measured by how well her son turns out. Without George's help she can't reach her goal, her security is threatened, and she therefore resents the obstacle, George. Let me see if her early memory confirms all this.)

"What kind of job did you do?"

Hazel: "Not too good. I didn't know how to hang up the towels and I made a mess of the sink with all the cleanser I used."

Counselor: (Most kids depend for security on parental reaction. I wonder how her mother responded?)

"What did your mother say when she saw the bathroom?"

Hazel: "My ears are still ringing. She shrieked, then tried to calm down but obviously was really upset. She

> even told me I was no help and to get out of her way."

Counselor: (I want to establish that the painful feelings of insecurity depend on criticism and rejection.)
"How did that make you feel?"

Hazel: "Awful, just awful. I wasn't sure if I hated her or me, but I was really upset. I went to my room and cried."

Counselor: "What need in you do you suppose was badly unmet at that moment?"

Hazel: "I don't know, the need to be appreciated, I guess."

Counselor: "Can I broaden it to say the need to be secure, to be loved no matter what?"

Hazel: "That sounds like it."

More discussion of childhood experiences, relationship with parents, feelings about self, etc. followed.

Counselor: "OK, Hazel, let me put all this together if I can. You have a basic need to be secure, like any normal person. But you were criticized quite a bit and a few times painfully like the time you cleaned the bathroom. That made you feel insecure. You learned that in order to feel secure you had to be accepted, to avoid criticism. Now in order to avoid criticism you had to do a good job. Doing a good job therefore became very important to you. You *had* to perform well so you could avoid criticism and thus feel secure. With me so far?"

Hazel: "I think so."

Counselor: "Good. You mentioned that a few people are talking about how poorly Peter is behaving and that tears you up because your security is threatened — you're being criticized. So you have to get Peter straightened out in order to avoid that criticism.

	Now think a bit. Whose needs are you trying to meet by wanting Peter straightened out — his or yours?"
Hazel:	"I can't believe it — but mine. I want him to be OK so I won't be criticized."
Counselor:	"And thereby feel more secure. Now you believe that Peter needs a better relationship with his father if he is to shape up. You have to get George to do his part to help Peter improve *so you can be secure.* But George is ignoring the whole situation. He is an obstacle blocking the path to your goal of getting Peter shaped up and thus feeling secure. Naturally you resent George because you really see him as keeping you insecure."
Hazel:	"Well, what do I do about this?"
Counselor:	"Hazel, finish this sentence. 'I will regard myself as a secure woman if . . .' "
Hazel:	"If no one rejects me."
Counselor:	"Yes, that's what you have been believing for years. How do you suppose the Lord would finish your sentence for you?"
Hazel:	"I don't know. I guess maybe you want me to say that I'm secure because Christ loves me."
Counselor:	"Yes. But don't say it lightly. Think it through. If you have been seen at your worst and eternally accepted by God Himself, then ask yourself — do I really need everyone to accept me? When they criticize me, is my security really threatened or does it remain untouched?"
Hazel:	"You mean I don't need Peter to shape up in order for me to be secure because my security doesn't depend on whether I'm criticized or not."
Counselor:	"Yes, exactly."
Hazel:	"I think I follow that but it doesn't help. I still feel angry."
Counselor:	"Of course. You haven't yet consciously practiced

this truth. You were nice to George when Phil was counseling with you but you still were telling yourself, maybe unconsciously, that you needed him to be different if you were ever to be secure. Can you commit yourself to the clear biblical truth that your worth as a person, your need to be unconditionally loved, totally depends on Jesus' love? Do you believe that?"

Hazel: "Yes, I do."

Counselor: "Good. Then here's what I want you to do. Write on a three-by-five card these sentences, 'I don't need Peter to shape up in order to be secure. I therefore don't need George to help me shape Peter up so I can be secure. I am secure, loved, and worthwhile regardless of what George or Peter do and regardless of whether people criticize me or not.' Now I want you to picture your mind as a tape recorder. You've been playing the wrong tape in your brain since you were five years old. The tape probably goes like this: 'I need to avoid criticism if I'm to be secure.' Put that sentence on a three-by-five card too. This week carry both cards in your purse. Whenever you feel either resentful toward George or worried about Peter, pull them out, read them both, reject the wrong tape, then repeat ten or twelve times the right one. OK?"

Hazel: "OK."

Counselor: (Next week I'll have her go back to all the good behaviors Phil assigned to her before, but this "thinking change" needs to become a practiced habit first.)

"Good. Don't expect to feel all that differently. You might feel worse at first. But you're filling your mind with truth just as Paul told us to in Philippians 4. 'Whatsoever things are true, think on these things.' We'll see you next week."

189

Counseling now has moved through Step 1 (identify negative feelings — resentment and anxiety), Step 2 (identify negative behavior — already accomplished with Phil), Step 3 (identify wrong thinking — "in order to be secure I must avoid criticism"), and Step 4 (teach right thinking — "my security depends on Christ's love for me"). Step 5 has been partly entered, securing a commitment to the truth established in Step 4.

The remaining steps include securing a commitment to practice truth (Step 5) and programing right behaviors consistent with right thinking (Step 6), which in this case will be a repeat of Phil's Level II counseling but with the crucial added dimension of CHANGED THINKING. Step 7 then will involve enjoying the development of love for George and patience with Peter. After the session just reported, which might in reality have taken up two or three sessions, counseling might continue for perhaps five to fifteen sessions before both counselor and client feel that substantial and permanent improvement has been made.

Summary and Conclusion

The local church should and can assume responsibility for restoring distressed people suffering from personal ineffectiveness to full, productive, joyful lives. In order to do so, it must develop its unique resources for counseling. In this book I have sketched a model for understanding people which suggests strategies for mobilizing and training counseling personnel from within the church to meet the needs of people. Three levels of counseling have been identified. Level I — Counseling By Encouragement can involve every member of the body in a meaningful ministry of profoundly helping one another. Level II — Counseling By Exhortation requires a number of people knowledgeable in Scripture, trained in interactional skills, and able to apply practically the wisdom of the Bible to living situations. Level III — Counseling By Enlightenment demands more extensive training but should equip its practitioner in less than one year to meet every nonorganic counseling need within the local church.

The entire model presumes two central concepts: (1) people desperately need meaning and love, or in the terms I prefer, significance and security. Most personal problems result from a deficit in one or both of these needs. (2) The Lord Jesus Christ is completely sufficient to fully meet both these needs. Biblical counseling seeks to help people more fully enter into the personal wealth that is theirs in Christ.

May God move us all to better convey by our lives and by our words that Jesus Christ truly is sufficient to the end " ... that in all things he might have the preeminence. For it pleased the Father that in him should all fulness dwell" (Col. 1:18,19).

Chart Appendix

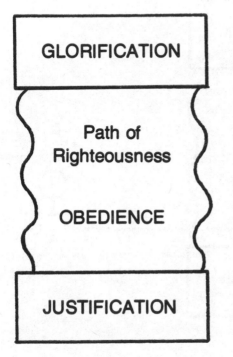

GLORIFICATION	I will be made perfect. God has predestined it.
Path of Righteousness **OBEDIENCE**	In view of my justification and my future glorification, I desire to please the Lord.
JUSTIFICATION	I am acceptable to God. He has declared it.

Chart 1 appears on page 25.

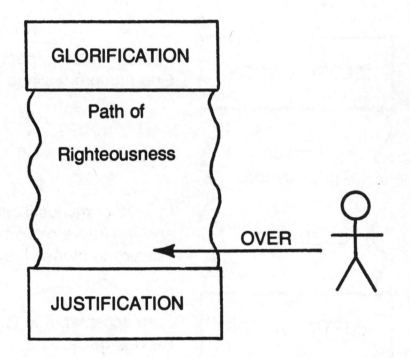

GLORIFICATION

Path of

Righteousness

OVER

JUSTIFICATION

Chart 2 appears on page 26.

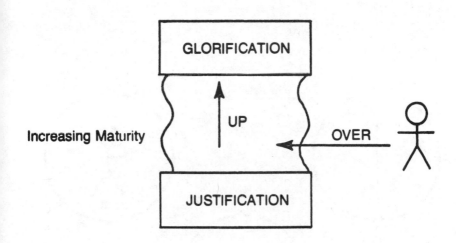

Chart 3 appears on page 27.

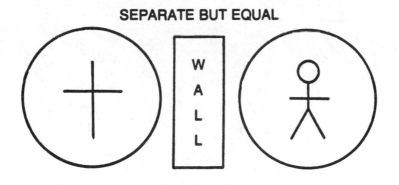

Chart 4 appears on page 33.

TOSSED SALAD

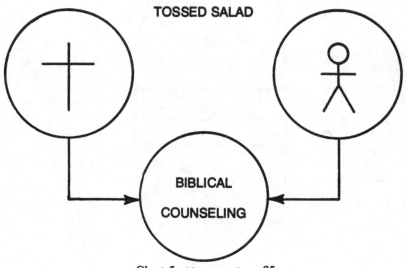

Chart 5 appears on page 35.

NOTHING BUTTERY

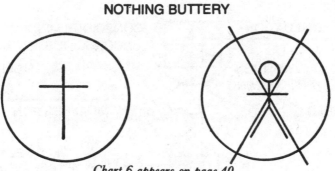

Chart 6 appears on page 40.

SPOILING THE EGYPTIANS

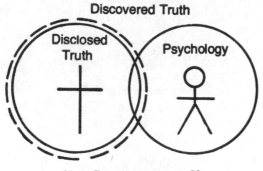

Chart 7 appears on page 50.

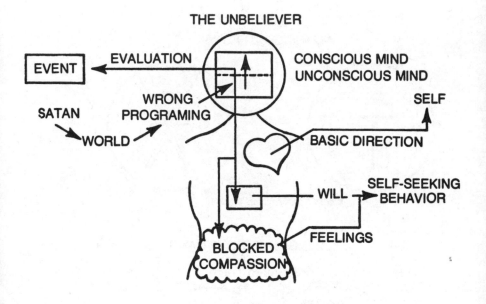

Chart 8 appears on page 106.

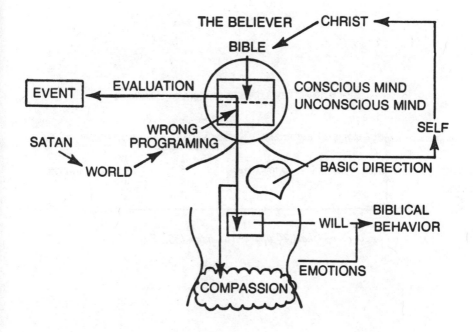

Chart 9 appears on page 107.

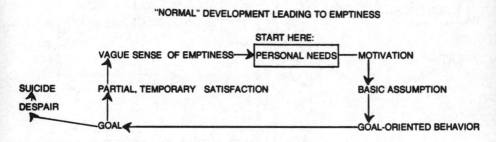

"NORMAL" DEVELOPMENT LEADING TO EMPTINESS

Chart 10 appears on page 136.

"ABNORMAL" DEVELOPMENT LEADING TO PSYCHOLOGICAL DISORDER

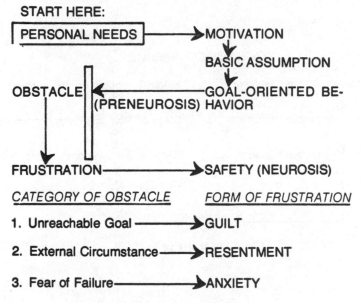

START HERE:

PERSONAL NEEDS ⟶ MOTIVATION

BASIC ASSUMPTION

OBSTACLE ⟵ GOAL-ORIENTED BE-
(PRENEUROSIS) HAVIOR

FRUSTRATION ⟶ SAFETY (NEUROSIS)

CATEGORY OF OBSTACLE   *FORM OF FRUSTRATION*

1. Unreachable Goal ⟶ GUILT

2. External Circumstance ⟶ RESENTMENT

3. Fear of Failure ⟶ ANXIETY

Chart 11 appears on page 136.

STAGES OF COUNSELING

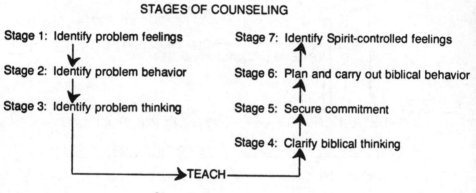

Stage 1: Identify problem feelings

Stage 2: Identify problem behavior

Stage 3: Identify problem thinking

Stage 7: Identify Spirit-controlled feelings

Stage 6: Plan and carry out biblical behavior

Stage 5: Secure commitment

Stage 4: Clarify biblical thinking

TEACH

Chart 12 appears on page 160.

LEVELS OF COUNSELING
Counseling by:

Level I   Problem Feelings——ENCOURAGEMENT———▶Biblical Feelings

Level II Problem Behaviors——EXHORTATION————▶Biblical Behavior

Level III Problem Thinking——ENLIGHTENMENT————▶Biblical Thinking

Chart 13 appears on page 165.